Imprisoned Fathers and their Children

Imprisoned Fathers
and their Children

Gwyneth Boswell and Peter Wedge

Jessica Kingsley Publishers
London and Philadelphia

First published in the United Kingdom in 2002
by Jessica Kingsley Publishers
116 Pentonville Road
London N1 9JB, UK
and
400 Market Street, Suite 400
Philadelphia, PA 19106, USA

www.jkp.com

Library of Congress Cataloging-in-Publication Data
Boswell, Gwyneth
Imprisoned fathers and their children/Gwyneth Boswell and Peter Wedge.
p. cm.
Includes bibliographical references (p.) and index.
ISBN 1-85302-972-6 (alk. paper)
1. Children of prisoners--Great Britain. 2. Prisoners--Great Britain--Family relationships.
3. Prisoners' families--Effect of imprisonment on --Great Britain. I Wedge, Peter. II. Title.
HV8886.G(Great Britain).B+
  362.7--dc21   2001053708

British Library Cataloguing in Publication Data
A CIP catalogue record for this book is available from the British Library

ISBN 978 1 85302 972 1

Disclaimer

The research referred to in this volume was undertaken by Dr Gwyneth Boswell and Professor Peter Wedge who received funding from the Department of Health; the views expressed in this publication are not necessarily those of the Department of Health.

In appreciation of our fathers
Philip Crisall 1901–1975
John Wedge 1902–1983

Acknowledgements

The study reported within this book was carried out under the Department of Health's Research Initiative on Supporting Parents and we should like to thank all those involved, in particular Dr Carolyn Davies of the Research and Development Division and Professor David Quinton of the University of Bristol.

Throughout we have received encouragement and valuable practical assistance from staff at the Prison Service Agency headquarters and from our research advisory group, Brenda McWilliams, Richard Nicholls, Janet Rich and Maxine Wood. We were fortunate in our research team membership: Sylvia Morley and Christine Williamson travelled the prison estate and conducted numerous interviews; Mark Barton provided computing assistance; Heather Cutting typed swiftly and patiently.

Finally we express our gratitude to prison staff and inmates, their partners and child carers, and the children themselves. They must all remain anonymous, but their involvement and willingness to share their experiences and views were essential to the research endeavour. We have tried to represent their stories faithfully in the pages that follow.

Contents

CHAPTER ONE

Setting the Scene

Introduction

All children, subject to parental absence, suffer from geographical and emotional separation. Prisoners' children are, in addition, frequently branded with a negative label, which customarily attaches itself to the partners and offspring of parents serving a prison sentence. They are themselves effectively 'sentenced' by virtue of their close association with the prisoner, to whom society has shown its most extreme form of censure. This same society, however, has a parallel duty to ensure the welfare of its children, notably by upholding their rights to maintain contact with both parents, provided there is no evidence of such contact being damaging to the child.

The prison population in England and Wales at 31 March 2001 was 65,394. Of this population, 61,842 were men and 3,552 were women (Home Office 2001). The prison service does not routinely include in its records information as to a prisoner's parental status, but estimates suggest that in excess of a quarter of a million children will be affected by parental imprisonment where the population is around the level cited above (Ramsden 1998).

The authors researched a large population of prisoner fathers, their partners/child carers, prison staff and children themselves during the late 1990s. Fathers became the focus because imprisoned mothers, who form a small minority of the population, have received considerable research attention (e.g. Catan 1989; Lloyd 1992b; Woodrow 1992) whereas the role of imprisoned fathers, rather like that of fathers in the wider population, has been relatively neglected. The findings from our study are employed, within this volume, to highlight and exemplify the issues to be addressed within the justice/welfare paradox that surrounds imprisoned fathers and their children.

Children's rights and needs

Within legal proceedings relating to parental divorce or separation, the well-known principle of the Children Act 1989 Section 1(I), that 'the child's welfare shall be the court's paramount consideration' is routinely brought into play. In Section 2(7), the Act further refers to the notion of shared parental responsibility, to which children are entitled, whether parents are together or separated. Additionally, in 1991, the UK ratified the UN Convention on the Rights of the Child (United Nations 1989). This states that children should be protected from any form of discrimination or punishment on the basis of their parents' status or activities (Article 2). It places emphasis on children's own views about their best interests (Articles 3 and 12), their right to maintain contact with a parent from whom they are separated (Article 9), and their rights to protection from abuse and neglect (Article 19). Further, the Human Rights Act 1998, incorporating the European Convention on Human Rights into UK law, now requires that the principle of respect for family life is observed (Article 8). Thus, unless a child is known, in some way, already to have been damaged by a parent, child-care policy in England and Wales assumes that the establishment and continuation of contact with both parents is beneficial to stable child development. There has so far been no evidence to suggest that this assumption should not apply as much to children and their imprisoned parents as to children and parents who are otherwise separated from each other. Nevertheless, it is rare for adult criminal proceedings to take into account either the 'welfare' principle cited above, or the likely effect upon 'shared parental responsibility' when sentencing a parent to imprisonment. Indeed, taken to its extreme, such a policy would render the majority of the convicted criminal population ineligible for imprisonment, thus seriously undermining the powers of the criminal justice system. Nevertheless, as in the USA where the prison population is steadily rising, the projection for England and Wales is for a continued increase, currently being provided for by an expanded prison building programme. Thus, the numbers of children affected can be expected to creep ever higher.

Earlier research has shown that families where a parent is imprisoned are likely to suffer significant disadvantages and to need additional and perhaps different support from intact families (Shaw 1987, 1992). Research in Scotland concluded that 'for most children imprisonment of a parent is a traumatic experience ... Feelings of loss and confusion may well be compounded by the altered financial and emotional resources of the remaining parent or carer.' As a result, 'the emphasis should shift from re-establishing family contact to maintaining family contact' (Peart and Asquith 1992, pp.21–22). Work by Richards (1992) and Noble (1995) leaves little doubt that children are frequently distressed, disturbed and confused, as well as financially disadvantaged, particularly by a father's imprisonment.

Other research has examined the role and importance for children of good contact between them and divorced fathers living apart from them (Lewis and O'Brien 1987) and for children in public care (e.g. Millham *et al.* 1986). Small scale research by the authors (Wedge 1995, 1996) has found that there are imprisoned fathers who welcome the opportunity offered by special schemes for visits by children, can make appropriate use of them and, in consequence, believe that their relationship with their child has been substantially improved. Partners also expressed similar appreciative views.

Evidence from child psychology research has shown that father involvement can be related to aspects of child development (e.g. Lamb 1981; Snarey 1993). An additional material factor is the impact of loss as such (e.g. Bowlby 1969; Lamb 1981; Lewis, Feiring and Weinraub 1981). A study of violent young offenders, in which both authors were involved, showed that 57 per cent of the sample had experienced significant loss in childhood, much of it parental and a substantial amount paternal. (Boswell 1996). Longitudinal research in the shape of the well-known Cambridge study of 411 London males has established a strong correlation (56%) between separation from parents (usually fathers) before age 10 and later conviction up to the age of 32. It has also shown that as many as 59 per cent of boys with a convicted parent were themselves convicted up to the age of 32 (Farrington 1995). These and other related findings, which will be further discussed in the ensuing chapters, also serve to emphasise the need for a much more comprehensive survey of current and potential arrangements for contact between imprisoned fathers and their children.

Prisoner fathers are, therefore, in some respects the same and, in other respects, significantly different from other fathers who are absent from the day-to-day lives of their children. Turning first to the similarities, it is necessary to begin by placing them in the context of absent fathers and fatherhood generally. What may any child expect from someone who provides 'fatherhood' in their lives, and what are the consequences for them of losing this facility from everyday family life, whether for imprisonment or any other reason?

The place of fatherhood in child-rearing

The legal expectation which 'shared parental responsibility' places upon fathers as well as mothers, in England and Wales, has already been referred to in respect of the Children Act 1989. This notion for the first time enshrined a gradually developing post-war view that traditional gender role divisions were outmoded and child-care responsibilities should be shared equally between the two parents. Arguably, however, this legislative innovation has produced a void in terms of any sense of distinction between mothering and fathering roles. Whether this is through intention or by-product, whether for good or ill, its effect has often been one of confusion and uncertainty about the current characterisation of fatherhood in modern society (Burghes, Clarke and Cronin 1997). This suggestion is reinforced by the fact that biological fathers who are not married to their children's biological mother have no legal parental rights but are nevertheless expected to support their children financially under the Child Support Act 1991. The position of young, unmarried fathers (who form a significant minority in young offender institutions and as young adults in the prison system) is of particular note in this respect (Speake, Cameron and Gilroy 1997). Often characterised in terms such as 'weakly socialised' and 'weakly socially controlled' (Halsey 1992, p.viii), their legal narrative appears to be the orthodox one of father as provider, while the right to participate in the physical and emotional role of parenting can perhaps only be bestowed upon them by their children's mother. To the extent that unmarried fathers, who are in a position to register their children's birth jointly with the mothers, may start to gain full parental rights under the provisions envisaged in the Adoption and Children Bill 2001, this situation has potential for improvement in the future. Overall, however, the legislative picture is blurred. It also tends to reflect a tension between the discourse of 'bad fathers' who don't support their children, drawn from the Child Support Act 1991, and 'good fathers' who share parental responsibility, drawn from the Children Act 1989 (Williams 1998). Is 'fatherhood', then, about financial support, about a true division of parental labour, about specific inputs to child-rearing which are unique to the male parent or, more esoterically, about the rights of children to some acquaintance with the male half of their origin and identity?

Generally speaking, traditional understandings of the fatherhood task tend to have been constrained by socialisation processes which taught and reinforced notions of the father as provider, father as disciplinarian, and so on (Barker 1994). Portrayals of fathers have not, on the whole, reflected images of intimacy with their children. As a result fathers were excluded from much of the early research into attachment theory, for example. It was Freud who set the scene for the mother as the primary attachment figure for a child. He described the child's relationship to her or his mother as 'unique, without parallel, established unalterably for a whole lifetime as the first and strongest love-object and as the prototype of all later love relations – for both sexes' (Freud 1940, p.188).

This was succeeded by Bowlby's work on maternal deprivation (1951), and his adaptation of this thesis centring around attachment and loss, and their effect on later emotional stability (Bowlby 1969, 1973, 1980). Other major pieces of research assessing attachment behaviours and outcomes all concerned themselves with early warmth, sensitivity and responsiveness towards the infant by the mother (Ainsworth 1979; Londerville and Main 1981; Waters, Wippman and Sroufe 1979). Rutter (1981) widened the attachment spectrum to include other 'significant' adults having, in earlier coverage of 'cycles of deprivation', reminded the reader 'that many different influences and different effects are involved and that these need to be differentiated if the processes leading to disadvantage are to be understood' (Rutter and Madge 1976, p.317). Lewis *et al.* (1981) also emphasised the father as a member of the child's social network which simultaneously satisfies multiple social needs.

Around the same time, modest studies in the USA were beginning to produce positive attachment outcomes in respect of single-father child-rearing experiences (e.g. Hansen 1986; Santrock and Warshak 1979). Later, Risman (1989) showed how situational opportunity could defy socialisation, to render single fathers competent as primary parents. Nash and Hay (1993) wrote of their findings in respect of the possibility of selective attachments with, for example, fathers or grandparents (though only if the mother was physically or emotionally unavailable). Howe looked beyond initial attachments to the significance of 'a matrix of social relationships' in the shaping of the secure child and the stable adult (Howe 1995, p.24). Geiger (1996) went further, confirming the arrival of fathers on the early childhood development front, with a publication entitled *Fathers as Primary Caregivers.*

From the mid-1970s onwards, however, a small number of researchers had also begun to pay attention to fathering styles which, arguably, constituted aspects of attachment for the child but still perceived any idea of fathers as primary nurturers and caregivers as limited by cultural images of fatherhood. Research by Richards, Dunn and Antonis (1977) in the UK and by Parke (1981) and Lamb (1987) in the USA indicated that, from an early age, play and physical stimulation generally constituted the main form of father–child interaction. (However, as Parke pointed out, this was culture specific and did not apply, for example, to Chinese, Indian or Swedish fathers). From his review of other North American research, Lamb concluded that fathers also played a major role in socialising their children towards moral, educational and cultural norms (Lamb 1981). Snarey (1993), continuing a longitudinal study of fathering begun by the Gluecks in the 1940s (e.g. 1945, 1968), found that the most common form of fatherhood involvement was in child and adolescent social-emotional development, though involvement in physical-athletic development was ranked second in childhood, decreasing in adolescence, and intellectual-academic development, ranked third in childhood, rose to second in adolescence. Notably, however, over a third of fathers were not really active in any of these areas of their children's lives.

Although significantly shaped by its social construction, post-war fatherhood did not remain static. From the mid-1960s onwards, fathers increasingly became welcome attenders at the births of their children; this and paternal participation in antenatal classes is now commonplace. As a combination of economic opportunity and changing social mores enabled mothers to re-enter the world of employment, the 'new man' began to emerge as someone who, theoretically at least, aspired to provide an equal share of the child care within an equal relationship with his partner. Over time, as one writer argued, the characterisation of fatherhood had shifted from 'moral teacher' to 'breadwinner' to 'sex role model' to 'new nurturant father' (Lamb 1986, pp.4–6). Recognition of the importance of equality in child-care responsibilities and its link to the labour market became enshrined in Article 6 of the European Communities 1992 Recommendation on Childcare:

> As regards responsibilities arising from the care and upbringing of children, it is recommended that Member States should promote and encourage, with due respect for freedom of the individual, increased participation by men, in order to achieve a more equal sharing of parental responsibilities between men and women and to enable women to have a more effective role in the labour market. (Council of Ministers of the European Communities 1992)

By the early 1990s, also, research on fathering in general was showing much more clearly that fathers wield an important and lasting influence on their children (Biller 1993; Snarey 1993). Importantly, Snarey's longitudinal work (1993), grounded as it was in Erikson's lifespan model of child development (Erikson 1950, 1959), also served to highlight the need to study parenting as it impacts on the range of psychosocial developmental stages.

Erikson developed the concept of 'generativity' – that is to say, caring for and contributing to the life of the next generation. Parents do this, he suggested, via creating and giving birth to a child (biological generativity), via child-rearing activity (parental generativity) and, ultimately, via the cultural obligation to help establish the next generation of adults (societal generativity). Later writers have argued that, although the social context may not always support it, active parenting is central to a father's growth and well-being and that inconsistency does not equal lack of interest or commitment (Hawkins et al. 1993). Hawkins and Dollahite (1997) have developed the concept of generativity and formulated the notion of 'generative fathering'. They argue that it is time to move beyond the 'deficit' model of manhood (Doherty 1991) or 'role inadequacy perspective' (RIP) which has often been applied to fathering as a consequence of abuse, absenteeism, emotional distance, lack of involvement in domestic tasks, and so on.

> The role inadequacy perspective leads to the argument that fathers perform the contemporary paternal role poorly. Yet the RIP's focus on glaring deficiencies often obscures the possibility that most fathers care deeply for their children and want to be good dads. We assume, and we believe this assumption is consistent with good research (e.g. Snarey 1993), that most fathers want to be good dads and many bring signifi-cant strengths to that work. (Hawkins and Dollahite 1997, p.8)

The exhortation here is to move beyond the traditional reliance on the metaphor of role, culturally determined and necessarily limiting, towards a concept of fatherhood as generative work; thus arriving at a broader theo-retical framework for the task of fathering in contemporary society. This also allows for changing life courses of fathers themselves, encompassing, for example, divorce/separation and non-resident child contact arrange-ments, remarriage/cohabitation and stepfatherhood, reversal/equal sharing of breadwinner/child-care responsibilities. Additionally, it provides a framework for understanding the way in which the task of fathering is transmitted from one generation to the next. According to Snarey's research:

> The greatest amount of unique variance in each of the different types of childrearing support is most generally accounted for by the characteris-tics of fathers' own fathers. These patterns suggest that fathers use childrearing to replicate the specific positive fathering they received and also to rework and rectify the specific unsatisfactory fathering they received. (Snarey 1993, p.304)

Snarey's work also confirms a much earlier finding about the influence of differential child-rearing experiences upon later parental behaviour (Stolz 1967). In the context of this volume, these studies point to the importance of considering the impact of imprisoned fathers' own experience of being fathered upon their fathering of the next generation.

Marsiglio (1995) adds three other theoretical frameworks to generativity, in an attempt to encourage researchers to consider the under-lying processes at work in fathers' developing understandings of their paternal identity as they move across the lifespan. These are identity salience (the extent to which fatherhood is important to their self-concept), commitment (to the fathering task) and univocal reciprocity (unconditional engagement in father–child exchange).

> Taken together, they contribute to an understanding of how fathers' participation in the negotiated, interpersonal relationship processes are related to their perceptions of and involvement with their children. Given the diversity of fathers' statuses and roles today, many fathers will experience multiple transitions involving their paternal identities throughout their adult years. Moreover, fathers will sometimes re-evaluate the relative importance and nature of their paternal identity in the course of these transitions, and express their commitment to it in various ways. (Marsiglio 1995, p.98)

More recent studies have confirmed the appropriateness of thinking beyond the fatherhood role and towards the actual nature of father–child interaction. Rounding up the available evidence, Burgess and Ruxton (1996) observed that many men are now both willing and able to move beyond the 'breadwinner' role to one of central involvement in child-rearing. Further, they concluded that the parenting styles of mothers and fathers are remarkably similar and that, once men take on significant levels of responsibility, their parenting approaches generally become indistinguishable from that of mothers (Burgess and Ruxton 1996). In a review of fathers and fatherhood in Britain, Burghes *et al.* chose to ask the question: 'What do fathers and children do together?' (Burghes *et al.* 1997, p.58). They cited O'Brien and Jones (1996), whose study of 600 East London 14-year-olds revealed that a quarter regarded their father as their favourite adult, and the person they would turn to first with anxieties about money, their mother and sport. This and a study of 8- to 15-year-olds by Ghate and Daniels (1997) highlighted the importance of fathers for young people and their desire to spend time together. As Burghes *et al.* point out, however, supplementary factual information about fathers is at a premium: 'informed discussion about fathers and fatherhood is hampered by an absence of regularly published official statistics. Unlike women, men who have children are not routinely distinguished in official statistics from those who do not' (1997, p.87).

Additionally, they call for more direct views and accounts of fatherhood from fathers themselves. This shortfall was addressed in *What Do*

Children Need from their Fathers? (Milligan and Dowie 1998). The reported research, based in Scotland, drew on cross-class groups of 58 fathers and mothers and 67 children in an endeavour to find answers to this question. Not surprisingly, these group interviews produced a wide range of material. However, in bringing together the respondents' perspectives, the authors concluded that there was no one quality or role which children needed from the fathers but that the reality was one of underlying subtlety:

> Without prejudice to the view that mothers can provide their children with more or less anything that fathers might give, at a more fundamental level there is still one need which it seems *only* a father can meet and this is not a truism – namely, *the apparent need of* daughters and sons to have a satisfactory and unproblematic relationship specifically with that one person who is, uniquely, their father. (Milligan and Dowie 1998, p.65)

The process of reviewing the main developments in the British and American fatherhood literature over the last half-century undoubtedly reveals a parallel with gradually evolving perceptions of what it means to be a father in a particular societal era. From being barely mentioned in pre-1970s childcare literature, other than as providers and disciplinarians, fathers' involvement in child-rearing has slowly come to be acknowledged initially via their presence at their child's birth, then via their play/ physical involvement, later through the child care/domestic sharing role and, more contemporarily, via the development of the generative fathering concept. It is important to recognise that any or all of these levels of perception of the place of fatherhood in child-rearing will be present in different living generations and that they may change across each individual's lifespan. It is necessary, also, to work within the 'zeitgeist' of current understandings, especially those which derive from the views of fathers, mothers and children themselves. What will this mean, therefore, for parents' and children's perceptions of the person who provides fatherhood in its unique (to them) form, when that person becomes absent from their lives for a sustained period?

Imprisoned father research

Imprisoned fathers and their children received little attention from UK researchers prior to the mid-1980s. The main reasons for this were that, as highlighted earlier, fathers as a broad category were under-researched and incarcerated prisoners' parental status was not and is still not recorded by prisons. An additional reason is probably that prisoners are an unpopular group in society, rendering the position of their children and partners anomalous and uncomfortable for the outside world (Davis 1983). *Sentenced by Association* (Blake 1991) and *Serving the Second Sentence* (Hardwick 1986) are significant ways in which two authors have chosen to entitle their publications about prisoners' families. This clearly is what makes prisoner fathers different from other categories of absent fathers.

An early exception to the paucity of research in this field was that of Pauline Morris (1965) who did not focus primarily upon children but studied the relationship between imprisoned men and their wives in a representative sample of 800 male prisoners from across England and Wales. She saw this as key to the adjustment of families to the temporary loss of their father and was, in fact, able to confirm her prediction that marriages rated as satisfactory before the sentence began would survive intact, this being largely a positive outcome for the children. Other early literature which covered the broad area of male prisoners and their families included Brodsky (1975) in the USA, Hounslow *et al.* (1982) in Australia and Fishman (1981, 1983, 1984) in Canada. All provided evidence of the benefits for parents and children of continuing contact during the prison sentence.

In 1987 and 1992 Roger Shaw published research material from a major study of two samples of imprisoned men received into a Midlands prison over two three-month periods. These men were aged 21 years and over and serving sentences of up to six months. Between them, the total of 415 men from the two samples were fathers to an estimated minimum of 584 children. Just under half were in stable marriages or partnerships at the time of their imprisonment and between them were fathers to 378 of the total 584 children (Shaw 1992). The other half were not living in a marriage or partnership at the time of imprisonment but were, between them, fathers to a further 206 children. From these figures and other surrounding factors, Shaw estimated that approximately 75,000 adult male prison receptions in England and Wales in 1984 could produce a figure of in excess of 100,000 affected children. This was before taking into account the children of young offender institution inmates among whom conventional estimates suggest that 35 to 40 per cent are fathers. Shaw further estimated that in excess of 500,000 children under the age of 16 at that time had experienced the incarceration of their father on one or more occasions.

Shaw's research showed, via interview and questionnaire, that children of imprisoned fathers tended to be socially, financially and educationally deprived, with the imprisonment itself exacerbating emotional and economic hardships. Families of fine defaulters, in particular, became prey to loan sharks pressuring them to buy their men out of prison 'for the good of the children'. Where Morris (1965) had found that 40 per cent of prisoners' children had not been told why their father was absent, Shaw found a figure of 33 per cent with a further 33 per cent who had been told lies. Alongside this lay problems of disturbed child behaviour, such as persistent truanting, running away from home, delinquency, bed-wetting, lack of concentration and deep-seated unhappiness, reported by teachers and health visitors. Less than 40 per cent of prisoners' wives and partners felt they had access to professional support from probation officers, social workers, health visitors, or the voluntary sector. As parents needing to support vulnerable children, therefore, they themselves were being left unsupported.

The second of Shaw's two books on prisoners' children was an edited volume which brought together views and research findings of specialists from various parts of the criminal justice system. Its aim was to spell out the plight of these children and to raise their profile as secondary recipients of decision-making in the sentencing process:

> It presents a challenge to those retributionists who attempt to ignore the unintended effects of an incarceration policy by arguing that the offender should have thought about the consequences. Such an ideology implies that it is acceptable for guiltless children to suffer if that is necessary for maximum general deterrence and public protection. (Shaw 1992, p.xiii)

Of particular note were continuing findings about the damaging effects of separation upon prisoners' children (Richards 1992) and the need for home leave to be granted more regularly (as happens in Sweden, for example) if it is to serve its original declared purpose of maintaining links with families (Walker 1992). To this day, home leave remains a privilege rather than an entitlement at particular stages of sentence. Other research has highlighted the financial and emotional burden upon families of male prisoners and re-emphasised the dearth of support available to them (McDermott and King 1992). Also, the particular problems faced by black or mixed race children of prisoners, including 'double jeopardy' on top of existing racism in the criminal justice system, the possibility of parental deportation, and deprivation of part of their cultural identity, were catalogued. In respect of ethnic minority youngsters:

> Many children find that having a parent in prison can seriously limit their access to cultural identity and understanding. Furthermore, some seem to have found that they encounter concentrated racism upon visiting a prison, especially where the prison may be located in a primarily non-black area. (Amira 1992, p.94)

These and other problems were further emphasised in a study of black and Asian prisoners' families (Light 1994). They raise issues which are of increasing importance in a situation where the percentage of black prisoners is both significant and rising (towards 25% in this country; towards 50% in the USA).

Other writers have explored the roles of the school (Moore 1992), the probation service (Wilson-Croome 1992) and prison visitors' centres (Lloyd 1992a) in relation to parental child support. These contributions demonstrated the lack of strong, consistent statutory policies which might support professional help in maintaining family ties, and showed that much existing good practice, notably in the provision and running of visitors' centres and crèches, emanated from the voluntary sector: this despite successive research findings that prisoners who do maintain strong family ties appear to be less at risk of reoffending than those who do not (Ditchfield 1994; Glaser 1964; Haines 1990; Hairston 1988; Holt and Miller 1972; Hostetter and Jinnah 1993; Leclair 1978). In a conclusion to his edited volume, Shaw deplored the 'profligate use of custody by the carcerial society' (Shaw 1992, p.194) and called for proper support systems to reduce the harm currently suffered by prisoners' children. He posed ethical and human rights questions:

> Does the state have a right morally – as practice shows it has legally – to strip a child of its parent because that parent has offended, although the crime may have been less harmful to the victim than imprisonment of the offender is to his or her child? Does not the child have a right to uninter-

rupted parenting at least equal to the right of the state to punish? (Shaw 1992, p.195)

Much of the parallel American research has also focused on the way in which these moral and children's rights issues are in harmony with the responsible parenting role of fathers who are incarcerated. Hairston (1988), in particular, has identified the preventive effect of family ties during imprisonment and has looked at the motivation of imprisoned fathers to resume their parental responsibilities (Hairston 1989). As in the UK, the parental status of prisoners in the USA is not generally reported in official criminal justice statistics and, again like the UK, up until the late 1980s little was known about the family characteristics or parenting views of prisoners. Hairston's questionnaire study of 115 long-term prisoner fathers found that, partly because of their long sentences, they did not see their children often but nevertheless had a commitment to the parenting role and wanted to improve their parenting skills. This included those who had been sentenced to death (5% of the sample), clearly a deeply distressing situation for a child and one with which, mercifully, the UK has not had to contend for many years.

Campaigns, programmes and policies

Interestingly, as has been the case in the UK (e.g. NEPACS 1997), research on this subject in the USA has often brought academics, professionals and lay people together in a campaigning approach to support the relationship between the imprisoned parent and the child. Hairston, a professor at the University of Illinois, was vice-president of the pressure group 'Parents in Prison' when her 1989 study was published. Additionally, a special issue of *Child Welfare: Journal of Policy, Practice and Program* (Seymour and Hairston, eds, 1998) devoted itself to the subject of 'Children with Parents in Prison'. This had emanated from another initiative by the Child Welfare League of America, entitled 'Children with Incarcerated Parents'. In his foreword to the special issue of *Child Welfare*, the Executive Director wrote:

> Children and families have long struggled with the difficulties created when a parent goes to prison. Until recently, though, parental incarceration has not been recognised as a discrete issue warranting study and concentrated intervention. It is our hope this special issue of *Child Welfare*

will raise public awareness about the impact of parental incarceration on children, stimulate discussion about how best to meet the special needs of these children and their families, and provide a resource for the child welfare community as it responds to the growing numbers of children made vulnerable by their parents' incarceration. (Liederman 1998, p.468)

The special issue devoted only three out of eight of its articles to the subject of fathers in prison, despite their majority status in the incarcerated population. (An estimated 1.6 million children in the USA have an imprisoned father as against 200,000 with an imprisoned mother). These articles drew upon policy, practice and research findings to highlight a number of important issues. First, Hairston reviewed evidence (e.g. Hairston 1995; Lanier 1993) confirming UK findings cited earlier in respect of both imprisoned fathers and absent fathers generally, suggesting that many imprisoned fathers, though now absent and not necessarily married to their children's mothers, had on the whole played some kind of nurturing/caregiving role in their children's lives before their imprisonment and wished this to continue (Hairston 1998). This piece also pointed to the fact that fathers were often left out of decision-making processes by welfare, school and other agencies surrounding their children and that imprisoned fathers were even more likely to be overlooked because of negative stereotyping. Yet their contribution is needed by their children:

> Their children and families have expectations of them as well, although those expectations are frequently limited or altered by the realities of prison confinement. The family roles and responsibilities of incarcerated fathers, however, are seldom the focus of institutional policies, scholarly research, or child welfare services. Few family-orientated services are provided for incarcerated fathers or their children and father–child relationships are generally discussed as irrelevant or simply ignored in broader efforts to strengthen families and promote children's welfare. (Hairston 1998, p.618)

In terms of increasing knowledge, as cited above, about the negative impact of parental separation and paternal absence upon children and the need to sustain meaningful contact between child and father during periods of separation, a crucial point is made:

It is relatively easy to see how some prisoners and families choose to forego regular visits to save themselves the embarrassment and helplessness associated with family contact under poor visiting conditions. The practical issue for fathers, however, is that parenting cannot be put on hold to be taken up 'when I get out of prison'. Children grow up; their memories fade or they create new ones through fantasy and imagination. When there is no contact to support an enduring bond, they begin to experience their parents as strangers. Such situations can lead to permanent, rather than temporary, severance of family ties. (Hairston 1998, p.624)

The differential impact of paternal incarceration upon children at various developmental stages requires particular awareness. A further article in the special issue of *Child Welfare* discusses the particular effects upon adolescent children (Weissman and La Rue 1998). These include coping with family deception and secrecy about their fathers' whereabouts (i.e. they may not be told the truth or may, in turn, be leaned upon to lie to others). They also include gender issues, so that 'acting out' behaviour (i.e. running away or truancy) was associated with imprisonment of fathers and 'acting in' behaviour (i.e. crying or withdrawal) with that of mothers. Where there is deception around parental imprisonment, this has been linked by other researchers to delinquency, aggression and other negative behaviour, probably resulting from children's inability openly to work through their feelings about the parent who has left them (Gabel 1992; Hannon, Martin and Martin 1984).

The opening up of UK research on imprisoned fathers and their children (Shaw 1987, 1992) and on imprisoned mothers (Catan 1989; Lloyd 1992b) coincided, to an extent, with prison disturbances (notably in April 1990) and their investigation by Lord Justice Woolf and Judge Tumim (Home Office 1991), commonly known as the Woolf Report. This inquiry made a number of recommendations in respect of family ties. These included increased home leave opportunities (subsequently, in fact, reduced by 40% by the Home Secretary, Michael Howard, in an announcement in November 1994); the serving of prison sentences, where possible, in institutions close to prisoners' home communities; increased prison visits; and the consideration of extended visits from children to their fathers, if current experiments with imprisoned mothers were found to be successful. This proved to be the case with the Holloway Prison scheme which operated all-day visits from children to their mothers, in relaxed play and leisure conditions, on alternate Sundays. In particular, evaluative work demonstrated positive emotional consequences for both women and children (Lloyd 1992b). Thus, the government responded with a series of measures to implement the Woolf recommendations, although as the Prison Reform Trust and the Howard League pointed out, many of the recommendations constituted existing Home Office policy which, in practice, had been ignored (Shaw and Crook 1991). In particular, as Lloyd (1995) notes, Woolf's recommendations on family ties merely served to reinforce Prison Service Standing Order no. 5:

> It is one of the roles of the prison service to ensure that the socially harmful effects of an inmate's removal from normal life are as far as possible minimised and that his contacts with the outside world are maintained. Outside contacts are therefore encouraged especially between an inmate and his family and friends.

It was in this climate of renewed interest in relationships between prisoners and their families that other UK studies began to take a closer look at the particular issues involved in this kind of parent–child separation. In respect of fathers, Caddle (1991) and Mardon (1996) produced relatively optimistic evaluative and practice-based publications respectively on the value of fatherhood courses, a significant number of which have been set up for young men serving sentences in young offender institutions. Despite prison constraints which sometimes impinged upon attendance, Caddle found that the young men felt they had learned new parenting skills and their attitudes towards parenting had changed as a result of doing the course.

Mardon's interim measure of success was based on long waiting lists, low drop-out rates and feedback from the inmates about the developments in their relationships with their children at visiting times. However, both authors acknowledged the need for a longer term follow-up of these relationships, a problem which had also been identified in similarly optimistic-sounding interim outcomes from parenting programmes in US adult male prisons (Bayse, Allgood and Van Wyk 1991; Hairston and Lockett 1987). More recently, in the UK, research by the Trust for the Study of Adolescence involved a follow-up, six months after release, of a third of young prisoners who had attended fatherhood courses. They found that where the men were still in contact with their children, they considered that they had retained a significant amount of the programme content and were finding it helpful in their post-release parenting role (Dennison and Lyon 2001).

There is, similarly, a lack of follow-up studies for adults who have completed prison-based parenting programmes. However, as with YOI fathers, the interim picture appears positive (Evans 1998; Millington 1998) and the issues and trends for both will be further discussed in Chapter 6.

In an article which traces the strong increase of voluntary sector groups and the decrease of the statutory sector, notably the probation service, in supporting prisoners' families during the 1990s, Codd (1998) argues that the punitive political and penal climate of this era has prevented research and inquiry findings being implemented by the penal services:

> Although families are recognised as playing a role within the rehabilitative process, in a climate of retribution families become part of the landscape of punishment of the offender for wrongdoing. Limitations on contact with one's family becomes part of the retributive experience. The 'permeable wall' between prison and the outside community envisaged in Woolf's vision of community prisons has failed to materialise…By implication, the response of criminal justice agencies to the needs of prisoners' families indicates symbolic denunciation not only of the offender but also of his or her family. (Codd 1998, p.152)

In the abstract, this probably represents a fair summary of the climate of the last decade in which relevant research has been published. It is not, however, to deny the part which has continued to be played by the statutory services. HM Prison Service Agency has been responsible for the installation of telephones across all prisons, a highly significant development in prisoner–family contact. It also published a major guide to help agencies for prisoners and their families (HM Prison Service 1995) and, during this period, set up a Family Ties and Throughcare Unit (re-named the Prisoner Communications and Family Ties Section in 1997) supported by the Consultative Group on Family Ties. Based on earlier guidelines compiled in 1996 by a group of voluntary and statutory organisations with visitors' centre co-ordinators, the Prison Service Agency also published a set of good practice guidelines for visitors' centres (HM Prison

Service 1998). The probation service, too, has been instrumental in providing pockets of individual and group support, for example, organising transport to prisons in some areas, providing a presence in visits rooms (Wilson-Croome 1992) and becoming involved in the provision of prison-based parenting classes in others. Although much of the research cited in this chapter would point to the central importance for these agencies of providing formal child and family support, however, it is clear that such provision is patchy rather than consistent, that their new 'correctional' focus points them in other directions and that, as long as this remains the case, the push for a support framework will continue to emanate, not from statutory agencies, but from individuals and groups centred around the voluntary and charitable sector.

Summary and theoretical perspective

The foregoing review of research and issues surrounding imprisoned fathers and their children reveals a number of pointers to explore further in this volume. Research in this specific field of parenting is relatively new. Its endeavours are not supported by the collection of official statistics on numbers of imprisoned parents and affected children. It has tended to attract charitable rather than statutory funding and, as such, has been steered by a range of interested individuals and groups, resulting in an accompanying campaigning approach. Prisoners' families tend to constitute a low income and low status group whose needs and rights neither receive routine consideration in the sentencing process nor merit systematic statutory support during the sentences themselves. Prisoner fathers' children tend to exhibit distressed behaviour. Unless there are other factors to suggest that children may be at risk of significant harm by being in contact with their fathers, the evidence would suggest that regular visiting and other forms of contact may therefore be beneficial and instrumental in reducing the children's level of separation anxiety. Measures which are likely to support and enhance such contact include prison visitors' centres, crèches, children's visits schemes, parenting/fatherhood courses, and school/teacher awareness. Support networks in some other countries have developed faster than in the UK but seem to be evolving similarly in terms of addressing research needs, policy and practice via a corporate interest group approach, along the lines of the US model described earlier.

The research findings and concepts which have been discussed in this chapter are located in the following theoretical perspective. Prisoner fathers have been identified as a particular category of absent fathers and, in order further to understand the meaning of this type of absence for affected children, the place and nature of fatherhood in child-rearing has been examined. In this context, Bowlby's attachment theory (1969, 1973, 1980) and its later adaptations have been drawn upon to show that fathers now have a role both in primary caregiving and later socialisation. The concept of role itself, however, has appeared to constitute a limitation on conventional perceptions of what a father might do or be. Where earlier research found fathers adopting a predominantly play/physical involvement role (Lamb 1987; Parke 1981; Richards *et al.* 1977), later studies, a minority of which included the child's voice, revealed the importance of fathers simply being the unique person they were in the life of the child (Milligan and Dowie 1998). This is a notion which makes allowance for the developmental changes through which both father and child may move during their lives (Erikson 1950, 1959), and for the broader theoretical framework of generative fathering (Hawkins and Dollahite 1997). Such a framework enables stereotypical 'deficit' models of fathering which might be associated with prisoners, for example, to be replaced with one which examines what these fathers actually do and feel for their children, and what support they might need to assist them in maintaining these relationships. Here, the concept of social support can incorporate the need of the prisoner and his community to avoid re-offending, with the help of strong family networks, while simultaneously providing a framework for helping children to cope with the temporary loss of their father. Drawing upon these understandings, the next chapter considers the current circumstances of prisoner fathers, describing the basis of our study, the types of contact available between children and their imprisoned fathers, and the characteristics and perceptions of the fathers themselves.

CHAPTER TWO

Characteristics and Perceptions of Prisoner Fathers

For the purposes of our study, 181 fathers were individually interviewed and a further 20 interviewed in a group setting. The individual interviewees were made up of 144 adults (i.e. those aged 21 years and over) and 37 young offenders (aged 17 to 21 years in this sample). The group interviewees were from a local adult prison offering children's as well as ordinary visits, a distinction which will be further discussed in Chapter 4. The prisoners came from a total of 25 geographically spread establishments catering for all categories of security. A total of 19 adult establishments and 6 young offender institutions (YOIs) was visited in order to obtain these interviews. At the time of arranging the research visits, fathers in five of the adult prisons and three of the YOIs had potential access to parenting courses; fathers in eight of the adult prisons, but none of the YOIs, had access to a children's or family visits scheme.

Identifying and contacting prisoner fathers

In order to identify eligible prisoners and partners/carers, the researchers liaised with the contact person at each prison, whose name had been provided by the corresponding prison region's area manager. With the exception of men who had attended fatherhood courses, contact usually began with the partners/carers at visiting times, either for ordinary or children's/family visits. Because the focus of the research was to see how various support systems aided fathering to continue, rather than to discover how many fathers were in contact with their children, the researchers usually approached people who were visiting with children. (However, on occasion, if numbers were small, visitors without children would be approached and this sometimes revealed that they did have children whom they brought at different times or to other types of visiting provision.)

In prisons where partners/carers had been interviewed at visiting times, the researchers were usually able to request interviews with matching inmates the next day, or to return to the prison soon afterwards for this purpose. A standard explanatory letter to both prisoners and partners was made available, although only a minority of prisons was able to distribute these prior to the interview. However, the researchers did not and could not expect the prison system to revolve around their interviewing needs and, despite the best efforts of extremely helpful staff, it was rarely possible to see the full complement of matching respondents. Reasons for this could vary from inmates declining consent to be interviewed, to being outside the prison on a working party, to having been called to a legal visit, or having moved overnight to another prison. Return visits by the researchers were not always practicable, though on occasion those who had moved were later picked up in other prisons. This situation, therefore, explains why inmate and partner respondents are only directly 'matched' to each other in 99 cases.

The group interview followed the structure of the individual inmate questionnaire, with the exception of closed questions about individual characteristics, questions about parenthood courses, and about their own experiences of being fathered, potentially too emotional for a group setting. Their answers are recorded where they lend confirmation or added insight to the data from individual interviews.

A growing number of prison establishments run fatherhood/parenthood courses of different kinds with a view to educating fathers or expectant fathers about practical and emotional aspects of fathering and about being a father from prison. In respect of prisoners who had attended fatherhood courses a request was made, either to the contact name given to the researchers or to course leaders via the named contact, for a random sample (i.e. every other name on the list of previous course participants on the assumption that this was unlikely to exceed 20 inmates) to be invited for interview. In the event, such a target was over-optimistic. As Caddle

(1991) found in her study of young men who had undertaken such courses, several had not completed them for reasons ranging from conflicting work or education arrangements, to release on parole or transfer to another establishment. Others who would have been eligible for the present study had finished their sentences and been released on licence. Thus at each prison where fatherhood courses were held, all those who had completed the course were seen. Out of the 55 course attenders, 13 had not yet finished the course but were intending to do so. Their responses, therefore, had to be understood in this context, but were thought to be more useful than none at all. Research work in prisons not uncommonly has to engage in compromises of this nature. In a way its tensions are symbolic of those experienced by families – relationship continuity versus prison security, the ideal versus the possible.

All interviews with prisoners began with the research purpose being explained and their informed consent being sought. This was only refused in a small number of cases, in which event additional eligible respondents were sought. Confidentiality and anonymity were assured. The early part of the interview contained a series of closed questions about age, offence, sentence length, release date, family members, etc. These served both as necessary quantitative research data and as an initial opportunity to relax into the interview. Inmates were then asked which children (i.e. age and sex) and partners/carers visited them and which children, if any, did not, with reasons. These data, together with material from more emotional and evaluative open-ended questions about their perceptions of fathering later on in the interview, form the substance of this chapter.

The quantitative findings are frequently presented in percentage form. While these figures accurately reflect the responses obtained, they should not be interpreted as showing detailed or subtle distinctions. Rather, they indicate broad similarities or broad differences within or between groups of interviewees.

Inmate characteristics

Inmates were serving sentences for a wide range of offences, though anyone convicted of sex offences or violent offences within the family had been excluded from this sample because of potential distress to family members. While the sentence length spectrum ranged from under 12 months to over 10 years, it was notable that just over half the adults were serving between 3 and 10 years, while 35 per cent of young offenders were serving in excess of 3 years. These figures raise the two themes of changing sentencing policy and the sustainability of father–child relationships over long periods of separation. It is clear that in recent years the 'prison works' policy and related legislation have produced longer and more frequent prison sentences than hitherto for those who commit violent, sexual and drug-related offences. Applied to the 30 per cent of adults sentenced for drug offences and the 29 per cent sentenced for (non-family) violent offences in this sample, there are clear implications for the future effects upon contact with children. Although it was to an extent in the nature of the sample that the majority of adult inmates (92%) had continuing contact with their children, whatever the length of their sentence, it is possible that others serving long sentences outside this sample may have similar experiences to the US sample of 115 long-term prisoner fathers referred to in Chapter 1 (Hairston 1989). These fathers did not see their children often, but were nevertheless reported to be committed to their parenting role and desirous of improving their parenting skills. It is also important to note that only just under half of the young offenders received visits from their children, either due to distance of the establishment from home, or (more often) because relationships with their mothers had broken down. Arguably, then, it is worth giving further attention to the notion of sustainability of relationship across sentence length.

All the prisoners interviewed individually were within two years of release, as far as could be determined, and half of all adults, and two-thirds of young offenders were expecting to be released within the next nine months. A relatively high proportion (85% of adults and 76% of young offenders) were also expecting to return to live with or close to their children. This is a higher estimate than earlier researchers have given. Shaw (1987), for example, gave just over 50 per cent and Richards *et al.* (1994) gave 68 per cent in respect of their total sample of men and women expecting to return to live with their children. However, the follow-up interviews of Richards *et al.*, with half of their original prisoner father sample, found that the majority had some form of contact with their children. Most of those who were not living with their children saw them at least every four weeks. Nonetheless it should be borne in mind that the higher percentages of those expecting to return home, within the research described here, are likely to reflect the study's focus on those who do have contact with their children and the nature of that contact (including 8% stepchildren in both adult and YOI samples). The figures may also reflect the implementation of the Children Act 1989 in relation to shared parental responsibility and, perhaps, a greater public awareness of the psychological damage which children may suffer if they are deprived of access to a parent with whom they have a loving relationship.

In terms of age characteristics, the range of young offenders in the sample is narrow (17 to 20 years as referred to above), the greatest preponderance being in the 19 to 20 category. The range of adults is wider, with 45 per cent aged under 30 years, 35 per cent between 30 and 40 years and 20 per cent over 40 years, these proportions being very similar to those in the Cambridge Project sample (Richards *et al.* 1994). Ethnic origin data for the present study include figures of 85 per cent adult/81 per cent YOI and 90 per cent respectively for white ethnic majority prisoners and their partners/carers; 5 per cent adult/3 per cent YOI and 2 per cent respectively for white ethnic minority respondents; 7 per cent adult/14 per cent YOI and 6 per cent respectively for black ethnic minority respondents. The number of the latter is less than for the prison population overall, although Home Office end-of-month statistics on prison occupancy do not report on ethnic origin, making it difficult to get an up-to-date picture. However, this relatively low figure may relate to less prison-based contact between black families because of potential racism in that setting, to education practices/parenthood classes not being sufficiently culturally sensitive, or to extended family child-rearing practices in which the father does not play a major part. Although no black respondents referred to it, the Moyenda Black Fathers Project, based in London and offering support to black fathers and running a ten-week parenting programme, provides a model of a facility which could usefully be extended to the prison setting.

Numbers and ages of inmates' children

Somewhat surprisingly, about half of fathers interviewed had only one child, though this also reflected the answers from 37 young offenders, for the majority of whom this was the case. Thirty per cent had two children and fourteen per cent had three. The remainder had between four and six children. Less surprisingly, inmates' children spanned the whole range from 0 to 18 years. A category of 'over 18' was included to allow for a small number of adult inmates' eldest children (8%) who were under the age of 18 at the time of their father's sentence. The highest percentage of eldest children (21%) occupied the 12 to 15 year age group. Young offenders' children were all under the age of 6; only one YO inmate had a family of three. Over half of all their eldest children were aged less than two years.

This contrast between the range of children's ages for adults and for young offenders is a reminder of the differing relationship needs of children at varying stages of development, and the differential abilities of young and mature adults to meet these needs. The numbers of early teenagers and infants under 6 years may suggest that particular attention is required in this respect.

Carers of inmates' children

The total numbers of children living in families interviewed for this research was 325 belonging to adult fathers and 46 to young offender fathers, giving an average figure of fractionally over two children per prisoner father, only slightly more than the wider UK population average. Inmates were asked how many of their children lived with their current wife/partner/ girlfriend or with an ex-partner, etc. Sixty-three per cent of adult inmates' children and 67 per cent of young offenders' children were living with their current partner, wife or girlfriend. Interestingly, this means that among both adult and young offender inmates about a third of the children were cared for by someone other than the current partner of the inmate – usually ex-partners or grandparents. Nine of these children (3%) were being looked after by local authorities (i.e. were 'in care'). Of these, one child was about to be adopted, apparently without any consultation with the young offender father. One inmate told us:

> My close family members include three children who are in a children's home because they were abandoned by their mum in 1995. They'd been fostered unofficially with a neighbour who didn't receive any financial help. When she couldn't manage any longer she went to social services who declined to register her as a foster carer and therefore pay her, so the three children went into care. The youngest two have settled more or less, but the eldest girl is reacting very badly. (Children aged 14, 10 and 5)

Of adult inmates 34 per cent reported receiving weekly visits from their children; 59 per cent saw them at least fortnightly. Others came less frequently for a variety of reasons, most often associated with travelling difficulties or distance. By far the majority of children visiting inmates were the offspring of the inmate and the visiting mother. Just 4 per cent of children who were brought to visit were the inmate's and not the partner's. It was also clear from interviewing the inmates that, in a number of cases, there were well-established relationships with members of the family who were legally or effectively their 'stepchildren'. On occasion, inmates spoke warmly of their relationships with these stepchildren of whom there were 17 in adult inmates' families, and already 3 among young offender families. Where visiting children were not brought by their biological mothers, this was usually done by grandparents or other relatives.

Inmates not visited by their children

Adult fathers in the sample who received no visits at all from their children numbered about one in twelve. In some cases, this was because the child lived with an ex-partner and was prevented from visiting by that partner:

> There should be some arrangement made in court about visiting rights such as in divorce cases. When you are in prison there is nothing you can do if your partner suddenly decides to stop bringing the children. I'd love to have regular contact but it's up to my ex when I get to see them. I've seen blokes in here whose wives have refused to let them see the kids and it's nearly driven them over the edge.

> It's a good punishment – a part of the punishment – being kept away from my son. He doesn't deserve to be punished. He's missing out – he only sees his mum – he needs both parents. You are cut off from your family – that's part of the punishment – but it's punishment for them too. I can't think of any worse punishment than being separated from your children.

> I have to forget that I am a father and that I can't see my child (aged 2 months) or I get depressed. It's impossible for me to forget – it has got so bad I have been to the Samaritans – I felt so sad – I felt like killing myself. They don't help you at all to overcome problems. You are absolutely powerless to do anything. The probation officer is useless – it makes me angry – it makes me want to be violent towards everyone –

want to hurt people. I hate her [girlfriend] for not bringing the baby –
but I know it's not her fault – she has to do as they [social services] say.
(Inmate was accused by social services of abuse but no charges were
ever brought)

The following quotes also illustrate the view of a small minority of prisoners who consciously decide not to see their children, believing, rightly or
wrongly, that the experience of visits may be more damaging for the child
than not to see their father at all.

> I would consider letting my children visit if improvements were made
> to make the visits less intimidating for children. I believe that staff treat
> visitors like prisoners and in some cases worse. As an example there was
> a son of a friend who was thoroughly searched; this was distressing for
> both mother and child, especially as the boy was mentally handicapped
> and had to be helped to undress. The child was very distressed
> afterwards.

> If the security searches weren't so intrusive I would let my children
> visit. The way the officers speak to the visitors and children is not
> acceptable. I wouldn't want my children to be spoken to like that. There
> is nothing for them to do if they come. My ex-wife wants to bring them
> but I don't want them to see me in here. I don't think they could cope
> with it.

In some cases the children themselves may not wish to visit, but this is rare
and usually based on a previous bad or traumatising experience of the kind
recounted here:

> One son of 17 years doesn't come because he had a bad experience at
> another prison. As they were leaving he was pulled out as it was
> thought that he was a prisoner escaping. We had to wait ages until all
> the prisoners were checked. He was also body searched. The
> experience was very upsetting and frightening for him. After that he
> became very anxious going through security and being searched. So
> now he doesn't come.

Among all young offenders, over a third did not receive a visit, in addition
to those who were otherwise not at all in touch with their children. This
meant that virtually half of young fathers did not see their children. A
range of reasons follows:

I don't want my son (aged 14 months) to visit. Prison is the wrong environment to bring children into. It's not the right sort of atmosphere to bring children into. I've asked my girlfriend and family not to bring him because it would have a bad psychological effect on him – seeing his father imprisoned.

I had weekly visits when at the previous prison but I was moved to [present institution] six months ago and have received no visits since. (Inmate aged 18 with a son of 2)

The older child is out of contact. The younger one visits. The younger one is with my girlfriend, his mum, whereas the older child is with my ex-partner. (Inmate aged 19 with 2 children aged 27 months and 11 months)

It is of concern that such parenting experiences as these young men have are prison-based. Because they are young and some have long periods in custody still to serve, their babies and infants will grow significantly while they are in prison. Although they may have some knowledge of their children with and through other family members, where there is little or no contact there is undoubted potential for psychological pain on the part of these young men, who are sometimes little more than children them-selves, and for feelings of abandonment on the part of their children who may have no idea why their father is not in touch with them.

Feelings about being a father in prison

Each inmate was asked how he felt about being a father in prison. Almost all their replies expressed inmates' sense of guilt or helplessness. Among the adults, 35 per cent said they felt 'guilty' or 'ashamed'; 15 per cent said they were 'gutted' and 20 per cent described themselves as 'helpless' or said that they 'can't be one'; 17 per cent were 'unhappy' and a further 8 per cent 'frustrated'. The group interview respondents, between them, reiter-ated this range of emotions. Inmates told us:

I try not to think about it; I look at a photo of [daughter] and me just before I was arrested and another recent one of [daughter] and see the time in between. I have to take the photos down sometimes, they are so upsetting. It's near enough terminated my relationship with my children, because when you are absent during their childhood they don't forget you, but they accept that you are not there. They cut out the pain.

Bad – real bad. I need to be out there making sure that my kids are being properly looked after.

Disappointed and angry with myself. I just want to spend time with her [daughter of eight months]. I wasn't allowed to be present at the birth; I felt very, very disappointed. I would really have liked to have been there.

It's very hard to be a dad from in prison. I'm on the outside of their lives looking in.

I've been thinking a lot about my son; I dream vividly about him at least once a week. (Inmate has not lived with ex-wife and son for seven years)

Terrible. [Daughter] was born while I was inside – I think that's when I first realised I was really in gaol. I was close to tears. I am pretty gutted about missing her birth.

A similar pattern occurred among young offenders, with almost everyone expressing feelings of dissatisfaction, dismay, guilt or helplessness. One inmate aged 21 had a son of 7 months, living with foster parents following an interim care order at six months because the child's mother was not caring for him properly. He told us:

I feel frustrated that I am in here and can't do anything. It's strange to know that I have got a child. It hasn't sunk in yet. (Inmate has apparently not seen this child and receives no visits from the child's mother)

Inmates were then asked a number of questions about their view of fatherhood and, again, what might be done to help them discharge these responsibilities. First, they were invited to suggest characteristics of the 'ideal father' for their child/children. A third of adult inmates and about two-thirds of young offenders responded quickly with comments such as 'not in prison'. This was also the main response within the group interview. Such a response was usually coupled, however, with other attributes of an 'ideal father' such as 'loving/caring father' (half of the adults and two-thirds of the young offenders), 'economic provider' (adults 17% and young offenders 38%), 'giver of (quality) time' (adults 22% and young offenders 16%). Some 13 per cent of adult inmates responded along lines similar to 'myself – I'm their dad'.

It is, perhaps, of note that inmates did not fit into a disciplinarian stereotype. Only 13 adult inmates (9%) and 2 young offenders (5%) mentioned a disciplinary role for their ideal father. They offered responses about an ideal father such as:

> Takes responsibility and exercises it democratically and gradually encourages children to do likewise.

> Would be constantly *there*, take time out to think about responses to them; allow them to be what they *are*.

> This sentence has helped me appreciate the difference between spending time with her and spending money on her.

Inmates were then asked about the match of themselves to the identified ideal, a match which was substantially confirmed. While 10 per cent of adults and 8 per cent of young offenders described themselves as not at all matching their ideal, 43 per cent of adults and 30 per cent of young offenders saw themselves very much as the ideal they had described; 34 per cent of adults and 16 per cent of young offenders said that they loved their children but were not there to deliver on the ideal father they had described.

These responses do not suggest that time in prison has been spent reflecting on ways in which inmates might have failed to match up to their ideal as fathers and concluding that there are major deficits to be addressed. Perhaps the interviewees were less than entirely honest about this, but given their general frankness about themselves this was not the impression gained by the interviewers. It is, though, borne out by answers to the question 'What could be done in prison to help you get nearer to this ideal?' to which 49 per cent of adults and young offenders answered that nothing could be done. This was often, however, because the inmate felt the responsibility was his own:

> Before prison – yes I tried to be an ideal father. Now, no, I don't match up because it's a strange situation in here. I love to see and talk to them but their mother is always there – it's not the same as having individual contact with each of them – it's also a conflict – to spend time sorting

things out with my wife. They often go off to the crèche. The girl sits on my knee and wants to get close – the two boys 'cut it out'. There is a distance that can't be resolved in a two-hour visit. I feel I need time to break down their awkwardness and feel comfortable. There is a lot more I know that they'd like to say but we are all inhibited in here. The environment isn't right. They just need to see that nothing's changed. I'm still Dad. In some ways as long as the kids don't forget who you are, it doesn't make any difference to them that I am in here. They know I haven't changed, I'm still Dad, I'm still there for them. As long as you don't do anything to shatter that, they will be OK. Their security is knowing that I am still the same, I still love them and I am coming back to them. As long as they know that then I can work on getting them back to stability when I get out.

Each inmate was also asked what could be done after release to help him get nearer to his ideal. Again, the answer given more frequently than any other was that nothing could be done (58% of adults and 43% of young offenders). Apart from this, around 13 per cent of all inmates and many group respondents mentioned help with employment.

Inmates' own experience of being fathered and its influence

Each inmate was asked about his own experience of being fathered as a child. For adult inmates, the most frequently mentioned characteristic was of the father who was an economic provider (25%). When this is coupled with those who described their father as 'supportive/giving' (19%) or 'loving/caring' (15%), it is clear that many inmates considered that they had a positive experience from their fathers, at least for a proportion of their childhood. To set against this, there were those who referred to stern discipline (14%), to physical abuse (10%), to abandonment (10%), to a father who was remote or gave no hugs (16%); 5 per cent reported witnessing the abuse of their mothers, and 5 per cent had experienced life 'in care'. Some had never known their 'real father' (6%), had been brought up by a stepfather (8%), or had no father figure in their life (5%). Some of the most telling responses appear below:

I hardly saw him as a child. We came over from [another country] when I was six and lived in two rooms – nine of us. He was a restaurant chef and had to work long hours to support us. We were very poor and had none of the things other children had. When I got to 13 I started truanting and stealing to get them. My father hung me naked upside down from the ceiling and beat me with a strap. I was labelled 'uncontrollable' and put in a children's home for three years. I've been in and out of prison ever since.

Dad was a typical Victorian – made the decisions, didn't want anyone to disagree. He took responsibility and was inflexible. He treated my mother oppressively.

My own mum was a 'battered wife' and father was in the RAF. His father was adopted at age four and raised by a dominant aunt. I was shifted around boarding schools. Father abused me emotionally, ignored me for three days at a time, and I could never live up to my father's expectations.

I don't really remember much about him – he was always in prison – remember going to see him. My parents split up when I was 12. He used to beat my mum up, I remember that vividly. I don't have anything to do with him now; it's my decision. I feel nothing at all for him. I never got any love from him and I was in care at nine years old – that says a lot about my family doesn't it? I feel very angry when I think about it – so I try not to think about it too much. I blame my father. It has made me realise the importance of a good upbringing. I want her to get all the love and care that I never got. I want her to get a good education and go to college.

I never knew him. I lived with my grandparents and called them 'Mum' and 'Dad'. My real mum met my stepdad, who's a real 'dickhead', and they lived across the road from us. I never knew who she really was because I thought she was my sister. My mother had two more kids and then suddenly, out of the blue I was sent to live with them. I didn't want to go. I detested the kids and him. I've resented it all my life. I hate my stepfather. After about three years I went back to live with my grandma; I still think of her as my mum.

Haven't a clue – I've never known him. I spent most of my childhood in Children's Homes and Approved School. I have very little knowledge about why this was – I don't know any of my relations, don't know who they are. All I know was that my mother had a long-standing illness and that's probably why she put me into care.

I came from a good home. My parents moved when I was 12. I didn't want to go with them so I stayed at a friend's house. I wanted to leave home as soon as possible. My father was violent and 'knocked the stuffing out of me'. This made me rebellious and the more I got hit the worse I got. I got everything I wanted financially. Wish I had gone with them now. I have lost touch with my mother.

A 'tough roughneck'. He worked on trawlers. He was away a lot of the time. I was in children's homes from about the age of 12 – I'm not sure why – my parents thought I was out of control but I don't think I was any worse than other kids. It was like going to prison – an initiation – from then on it was Borstal – then on to burglary and prison. I think my mother just could not cope with six children with my dad away all the time.

I learned nothing from him. He was a tyrant, brutal. Physically abused me and my sisters almost daily, usually with a belt. [He was an alcoholic.] On one occasion he broke my cheekbone and I had to go to hospital. My father sometimes tried, took me fishing, showed me his greenhouse, etc. He was physically abused by his own father who died when my dad was eight.

Among young offenders the picture is less comprehensive because of the smaller numbers involved, but again the largest single proportion refers to father as an 'economic provider' (22%); 'loving/caring' was mentioned by 11 per cent and a 'supportive/giving' father by 8 per cent of young offenders. Among the more negative aspects, 14 per cent mentioned that they had been 'abandoned', 11 per cent that their father was remote or gave no hugs, 14 per cent had a father who had been in prison and 11 per cent had themselves experienced life 'in care'. In the event, 8 young offenders (22%) reported having a stepfather, a comparable figure to that among adult inmates (21%).

The experience of stepfathering was also the subject of interview. The findings suggest that while economic provision and other positive attributes were familiar to some inmates, physical abuse was also the experience of around a quarter of both adults and young offenders in this group. One inmate who had had a stepfather told us:

Never knew my real dad – he left home when I was one. I was a war baby – an accident probably. He probably took one look at me and didn't want to hang around. I keep thinking about him and wondering why he went. I found out when I was 14; up till then I thought my stepfather was my real father. I haven't been able to speak to my stepfather since – I couldn't face him – I can't even now. My stepfather never gave me any love. I caught my stepfather having sex with his daughter (my stepsister). My mother knew deep down but she wouldn't believe it was true. She stayed with him but she now makes his life hell. It went to court and he got probation. Since I have been in here I keep thinking, 'Why did my father leave me?'

Influence of their own fathers upon inmates' fathering styles

The general impact of these experiences of being fathered was reflected in the responses of inmates to questions about this. Only 9 per cent of adult inmates and 5 per cent of young offenders suggested that their own experience of being fathered had no influence on the way they fathered their own children. Against this, 26 per cent of adults and 22 per cent of young offenders said that they would do the same kind of thing as their own father, reflecting positive aspects of their father's behaviour. For example:

Yes, he is a great father. I want to be like him. I had a very happy childhood and good family life. I want my children to have that. I want to make sure they do.

The largest category of response, however, was of those who said that they would do the opposite of the negative aspects of their father's behaviour towards them, in bringing up their own children. As many as 44 per cent of adult inmates and 49 per cent of young offenders responded in these terms. For example:

I realised when in here that I was doing things like my father did. There was a communication barrier. Gradually I have changed that – read, helped with diagrams. I ask about school, and friends. There's more communication which is better for both. She seems better for it. I had a father in the house but didn't know him. I want my daughter to know me. I'm more considerate now and more supportive emotionally.

Yes, I want to have a better relationship with them than I did with my father. I want to be there for them – to listen to them – they give me brilliant moments. I want to do everything I can for them.

I am and would be the complete opposite. Never hit my daughter. Give her lots of love, hugs and kisses. Got this myself from my mum which is how I stay cheerful.

I learned a lot – particularly the overriding responsibility materially. But I now see that it's not enough. The relationship course has made me see that – with terrible clarity. Not a pleasant realisation.

I do my best to give them everything I never had. I have never laid a hand on either of them. Because of what happened to me, I won't let them stay with their mother when her boyfriend is around. I don't want them to see things that children shouldn't see.

I know how important a fatherly role is from the parenting classes here, and I don't want him to grow up like me without a father.

This suggests that although there were many positive experiences during childhood for some inmates interviewed, a high proportion of them reflected on poor and/or painful experiences in their own lives which they were concerned should not be repeated. This made their broader reflections on the subject of their own ability to father from prison of even greater concern:

You are not a father at all when you are in prison. You are not there to help if they are ill or hurt. They take away every liberty you have when you are in prison, including fatherhood. Weekend imprisonment would be good. I would be at home Monday to Friday. Visits should be any day you want and as many as you want. If there's a problem and you have to wait a week, people just feel distressed for that period and the problem is exacerbated. Travelling is problematic at weekends but weekdays it's problematic for schooling.

You are not a father when you are in prison. You are just a stranger to them in the end. If you have a good partner and they are willing to bring the kids to visit it might be OK – but then it's not a very good environment to bring them to – and when they have to leave it's terrible to take them away from someone they love. It's important for kids to have both parents but attitudes in society have changed, they're less moral. The trend towards one-parent families is wrong. It has a bad effect on kids – they only get love from one parent and they suffer financially too. They should do more in prison to make it easier for men to stay in contact with their children. Many wives just stop visiting because it's too much hassle for them. (Inmate has two sons aged five and six and last saw them two years ago; his girlfriend is now in a new relationship)

You can still encourage and love them, even from here.

It's hard work. I wouldn't have [son aged five] visiting me even if I could because 1, I don't want [son] to see or remember me in prison and 2, this might set a bad example because [son] might think it's something good. (Inmate has no contact with son who is living with inmate's ex-girlfriend)

The eldest boy failed his 11-plus pre-test despite being very able. I feel this is due to the stress of having a father in prison. The seven-year-old daughter misses her dad; she was very close to me.

If I had been a father before the crime I would never have done it. Fathers need to be with their children. It's harder for young offenders because no one considers you as a father. They certainly don't take that into consideration when they sentence you. You get no support in the fathering role in here. They just think you are irresponsible for having kids in the first place.

Don't be a criminal if you want to be a father.

Added to these generally negative self-images were also the inmates' views of the effects of their imprisonment upon their partners' and carers' parenting role.

Effects on children's mothers/carers

Only a small minority of inmates considered that there had been no change in the role. Very many referred to life being 'harder for her' (51% of adult inmates, 41% of young offenders) and to their partner having 'to be mother and father' (32% of adults and 14% of young offenders). Some 13 per cent of adults mentioned that their child/children played their mother up. Among the adults, 12 per cent considered that their imprisonment had made their partner strong or more independent, but 9 per cent referred to her 'not coping well'. The group interviewees expressed a general view that the prison sentence was worse for their partners than for them. Although they had lost their freedom they were in many other ways free of the anxiety and difficult decision-making that goes with life on the outside. There was a high recognition that life was difficult for their partners, having to cope in a single-parent fashion, often on low income, and also needing to find the resources of finance and energy to visit the prison, usually with their child/children. For example, inmates said:

> She's having a hard time coping with three little children, losing the house (repossessed as a direct result of conviction). She's as strong as an ox but gets stressed at times. When it's ' women's week' she gets depressed and the kids start 'doing her head in'. She needs lots of hugs and support then – which I can't give – not even at visits. All I can do is hold her hand – and then it's at a distance, stretched over a table. She now lives with her mum and dad which isn't easy.

> She couldn't cope with me being in prison. It put too much strain on the relationship. We have split up since I've been in here. Of course, it's changed her role because she is a one-parent family now. It's been very hard for her having to do everything on her own. She developed a drug problem and has become disorganised and does not cope well. I tried to organise lifts for her to come with the children but she nearly always lets the lift down.

> It's been very hard for her. We live in a small community so there's lots of stigma. My wife is [a professional] which has been difficult for her. She has to work full-time as well as look after the children. It's been a terrible time for her.

> It's made a great difference. She has had to move back in with her parents [because of physical limitations on her]. I used to do lifting, washing, and many practical things. She had to get her parents to support her disciplining and controlling the children but, as her mother doesn't like me, she is using her support for her daughter to control contact with me. So my mother-in-law is a powerful, negative influence on the family.

Effects on children's behaviour at home

When each inmate was further asked for his view of the effect of his imprisonment on his children at home, less than a third reported more difficult behaviour, 8 per cent that their child had become anxious or withdrawn, and small numbers reported that their child was receiving professional help, wetting the bed, or in one case becoming violent. These figures were broadly borne out by partners' responses. However, those whose children had been notably affected gave some of the following examples:

We've lost our home, my job and now have nothing. At home the oldest has started smoking (aged 14), has been drunk a few times, has smashed her bedroom at the children's home, has run away three times, has shoplifted when drunk. The younger two are still OK at school according to reports. The eldest (aged 14) was excellent, but is now really bad.

Daughter (10) keeps getting into trouble at school. In one incident the police were involved when a child had smashed a window at school. She doesn't listen to her mother, is very disobedient, and plays her mother up constantly. She is a bit confused because of what's gone on. I don't know what's in her mind. I know she has heard things said about me from her grandparents.

She's been very affected. She has said lots of things to my wife, such as 'Why has Daddy gone away?' She cries in bed at night and keeps saying repeatedly, 'I want to see Dad', 'I miss Daddy', 'Please don't argue!' It upsets my wife, it upsets me. She's confused, she can't understand where I am or why I am here. She thinks I am still at court, but 'a big court'.

There's been a psychological effect. My three-year-old son understands a lot, but is confused and doesn't really believe it when I say I'm coming home soon. I tell him to be a good boy for his mum but I don't ever tell him off. I feel I don't have the right when I am not there to be with him. He says, 'I have been ill three times and my dad hasn't come to see me once.' It seems he has also remarked that other kids' dads take them out and his doesn't.

My kid was upset before my sentence because she was worried, and her work suffered. Now she's doing much better.

My daughter (aged 9) gets me to speak to her friends on the 'phone to prove that she has got a dad.

One child was quite badly affected. He started to sleepwalk and was found out in the street one night. The youngest child [aged 7] daydreams a lot to the extent where she appears to be in another world a lot of the time. We feel this is not normal behaviour. She has also become clinging and doesn't want to be left with babysitters or other family members.

Plans for father–child contact on release

In the light of some inmates' concerns about the effect of their incarceration on children at home, and of most of them about their ability to be fathers from prison, the researchers questioned them about their plans for their fathering role on release. When asked if they would be going home to live with their child/children on leaving prison, just under 70 per cent of adults and 60 per cent of young offenders reported that they would be doing so. Of the others, some 16 per cent reported in each case that they would not be going to live with their children at home but would be close at hand. A few adult offenders stated that they would be distant from their families and a proportion of adults (8%) and of young offenders (11%) did not know what their living arrangements would be on release. However, the figures of those planning to return home and/or remain in close contact with their children (85% for adults and 76% for young offenders) highlight the importance for these fathers of sustaining and, if possible, enhancing relationships with their children during the imprisonment itself.

Inmates were also asked what it was they were looking forward to doing with their children on release. Many responded that they wanted just to be with their children (56% of adults and 51% of young offenders). Some also looked forward to playing with their children (adults 21%, young offenders 24%), going for walks and playing in the park (adults 23%, young offenders 38%), or taking holidays (adults 19%, young offenders 5%). Only small numbers of inmates referred to 'supporting' their children or 'helping them with their school work' or 'providing for them' as activities to which they were looking forward. Perhaps not surprisingly, respondents concentrated on practical rather than abstract expressions of their return to their children, since these were the activities which prison, for the most part, prevented them from engaging in.

In summary

This chapter has highlighted the issue of sustainability of father–child relationships in the light of increasing sentence lengths for drugs or violence, offences of which nearly 60 per cent of adult inmates in this study had been convicted. It has also identified a particular problem, especially for YOI fathers in this sample, of lost contact with their children, often as a result of fragmented relationships between youthful partners. However, this does have to be balanced against examples of visiting contact outlined in Chapter 5 which show that complex relationships between young partners need not mean the loss of the father–child relationship.

On the positive side, a very high proportion of the adult prisoners (92%) received visits from their children, and the vast majority of all prisoners expected to be living with or near their children on release, and mainly looked forward to being with them or playing with them.

Apart from young offender fathers, the age range for prisoner fathers appears unsurprising. However, the low percentage of black ethnic minority prisoners (proportionate to the population) and partners is worthy of note and investigation to see whether black parents are receiving equivalent support systems to white parents.

It is clear that many prisoner fathers have low self-esteem about the effects of their incarceration upon their children and partners/carers, and other research has found that there may be a danger of this leading to diminished contact over time. Very importantly, however, these prisoners confirmed the findings of other researchers in their desire to reproduce positive aspects of their own fathering and do the opposite in relation to negative aspects. This is not only encouraging for the health of the next generation, but also requires further exploration of the effects of father absence upon children, which in turn requires that the voices of the children themselves should be heard. These matters form the subject of the succeeding chapter.

CHAPTER THREE

The Effects of Father Imprisonment upon Children

Research on absent fathers has generally focused upon contact following parental separation and divorce. However, it is possible to extrapolate from this some of the key factors which are relevant to children and fathers separated by imprisonment. This chapter will begin with a review of relevant literature and move on to hear the views of mothers/carers and then children themselves about their continuing relationships with their imprisoned fathers.

Non-residential fathers

A much-quoted statistic, taken from a study of lone-parent families in the UK, is that 40 per cent of fathers separated from their children are completely out of contact with them after five years (Bradshaw and Millar 1991). This has been dubbed 'the 40 per cent rule' (Burgess 1997). However, it may be that survey inconsistency between lone mothers and non-resident fathers has produced an overestimate in this figure, and subsequent surveys have reduced this percentage to as low as 25 per cent. The work of Simpson, McCarthy and Walker (1995) suggested that non-residential fathers fell into two distinct groups: those who were resigned to the situation and those who remained angry and bitter. None liked being in this position and the reasons for their lack of contact with their children were usually complex.

Outcome studies of the separation of children from non-residential fathers following divorce have produced a range of findings, generally suggesting that continuing contact is beneficial to the child's development, while loss of contact is frequently damaging. It is important, here, to make the distinction between permanent loss through death and temporary or permanent loss through separation, the adverse effects on children being significantly less in the former situation (Ferri 1976; McLanahan and Sandefur 1994; Richards 1987). Looking at academic performance, for example, Bisnaire, Firestone and Rynard (1990) found that 30 per cent of children in their study showed a marked decline over the three years following parental separation. Better academic adjustment was present in children with continuing access to both parents, and non-residential parents (mostly fathers) remained very influential in their children's development. The more time they spent with the non-residential parent, the better was their overall adjustment. Similar results were found by Drill (1986) in relation to young adult children's sense of loss. Where the non-residential parent (again usually the father) was perceived as 'lost', the young adult was found to be more depressed. Continued involvement with this parent appeared to be crucial in preventing an intense sense of loss in the child. Additionally, in a study of children in the mid-western USA, father loss through divorce was found to be associated with diminished self-concepts in children (Parish 1987). Intellectual and psychosocial adjustments tend to vary somewhat across sex, class, race, culture and at critical child development stages (Johnson 1997). Research samples have tended to be small and focused on low-income children. Nevertheless, in reviewing the available literature, Johnson is able to conclude:

> Fathers are important as parents; however, complete or optimal parenting is not limited to a particular familial structure. Rather, certain childrearing objectives and socialization strategies and goals must be in place. Optimal parenting may be defined as the rearing of a child in a nurturing, loving and safe environment where skills and ideals are engendered that enable the child to be a whole, contributing member of society. Using this definition, many family configurations, irrespective of parental resident of either gender, can achieve this end if given proper support. (Johnson 1997, pp.18–19)

Quoting a range of 1980s longitudinal research studies in the USA, Ihinger-Tallman, Pasley and Buehler (1995) hypothesise that existing low or significantly reduced role identity following divorce will affect the extent to which a non-residential father remains involved with his child. Several small-scale studies have offered potential explanations for this (e.g. Ahrons 1983; Kruk 1991). More recently Arendell (1992, 1995) has confirmed these earlier findings which, via in-depth interviewing of non-custodial fathers, point to 'gatekeeping' behaviour by mothers which moderates the relationship between fathers' role behaviour and father–child involvement. Thus, if the mother has a high regard for the father's parenting abilities, she is likely to encourage and facilitate regular contact, whereas, if her regard is low, the contact is likely to be weakened and may, at times, be sabotaged. It is not unusual either for payment of child support to become an instrument for battle in relation to access to children (Arendell 1995; Bertoia and Drakich 1993). Where non-resident fathers are unemployed, this is likely to become even more problematic (Braver, Fitzpatrick and Bay 1991), and the combination of low provider status and low regard of parenting skills may well lead to the reduction of self-defined role identity, which Ihinger-Tallman *et al.* (1995) suggest can result in diminishing or total loss of contact with the child. In respect of fathers in prison, one writer refers to a tendency for them to withdraw their interest in the outside world:

> It is as if, because the father has no real power, imprisonment destroys or damages the paternal image for both the father and the child. Families commented that their relationships were adversely affected by prisoners' growing loss of interest in outside matters over which they had no control and by their increasing emotional inaccessibility. (Pope 1987, pp.93–94)

Equally, it is not difficult to see how the mother's 'gatekeeping' role, with its surrounding influences, can relate very critically to the level of continuing contact children have with their imprisoned fathers.

Other obstacles to continuing non-resident father contact with children include rejection of the father by the child (Greif and Kritall 1993), though this is complex and may well include other factors such as maternal and extended family influence. These difficulties, with the addition of geographic distance, were cited by Minton and Pasley (1996) in their comparative study of non-divorced and divorced non-resident fathers. Catan, Dennison and Coleman (1997) also found children's increasing independence in adolescence reflected in reducing levels of contact and communication between young people and non-resident fathers.

Teenage fathers

Within the broad categories of 'non-resident' or 'absent' fathers, teenage fathers can frequently be found. Like their female counterparts, they may be contending with the interruption of education/career and with economic disadvantage. Importantly they are also facing the dual demands of completing a major phase of human development on the one hand and, on the other, societal pressures to occupy an adult role with its attendant expectations of breadwinning, responsible conduct, and so on. In reviewing the limited research on these young men, Rhoden and Robinson (1995) point to the fact that until the 1980s they were largely excluded from studies on adolescent parenting and, additionally, tended to be subsumed into the general literature on parenting, much of it prior to that period derived from women respondents. However, more specific findings from subsequent research, they argue, challenge the 'stereotypical villainous stud' who sexually exploits young women and then abandons them and their offspring (Rhoden and Robinson 1995, p.107).

This last sentiment reflects a deficit perspective on young fathers which, it is suggested, leads society, including responsible professionals, to exclude them from involved parenting from the outset. This comprises lack of choice in decision making about pregnancy termination; banishment by angry parents of pregnant girlfriends; hostility from courts and child support agencies. This may engender greater likelihood of lifelong father–child separation on the basis that to re-establish what was once present is liable to be easier than establishing, for the first time, something which never previously existed. However, while some teenage fathers nevertheless appear to fit the stereotype (as portrayed, for example, in Blankenhorn 1995; Dennis and Erdos 1992), Rhoden and Robinson (1995) conclude that most do not. For example, one study found that physical or psychological involvement by teenage fathers endures throughout pregnancy and childbirth (Kiselica, Rotzien and Doms 1994).

Interviews with 289 adolescent mothers showed that teenage father absence did not necessarily mean lack of involvement; indeed they were judged to be more involved with their children than adult fathers (Danzinger and Radin 1990). In a national survey, 227 men who first fathered as teenagers reported greater parental satisfaction than did older fathers (Heath and McKenry 1993). Thus:

> We are learning that the stereotype of teenage fathers as uncaring and uninvolved males is not always true and that given the chance, many of them report that the fathering experience is a central event in their young lives. Many teenage fathers are emerging as young men who want to be active fathers. (Rhoden and Robinson 1995, p.106)

Clearly, teenage paternity is a category within the fatherhood umbrella which requires careful consideration in terms of the quality and quantity of support provided from the outset if sustained child–father contact is to be an aim.

Physical and psychological absence

It is clear that as non-resident parents, absent fathers are faced with a variety of social, financial, geographical, emotional and developmental difficulties in maintaining a relationship with their children. The shortage of studies taking careful account of these factors has made it difficult to be specific about the effects of father absence upon children, particularly since the children's own perception of the reasons for their fathers' absence is likely to be key to this area of understanding. There are also some grey areas surrounding known or potential damage to children from certain kinds of behaviours by fathers.

Two particular situations that may be seen as pointing to the desirability of father absence are those in which children have received or witnessed paternal violence or abuse, and those with fathers who have offended, given the established association between a father's criminal record and later delinquency in his children (Rutter and Giller 1983; West 1982). Even here, however, the picture is more complex than it seems. First, separating a child from a violent or abusive parent may serve a protection requirement but not a care requirement (e.g. Parton and Parton 1989). Children may continue to love and wish to have contact with this parent within some form of protected environment. Similarly, as Farrington (1995) has shown, certain types of parental discipline, supervision and attitude (e.g. excessively harsh or inconsistent discipline, or failing to monitor children's whereabouts and activities, or not providing warm and loving contact– whether occurring singly or in combination) are the best predictors of subsequent delinquency. Again, the fact that a father provides, in part, a negative role model does not necessarily imply that he cannot simultaneously offer some of the positive aspects of fathering which are of value to the child. As Milligan and Dowie (1998) show, although children in their study talked most about their need for a role model, they were aware that this involved both positive and negative aspects. They also expressed their need for quality time, supportive behaviour, expressions of love and physical contact from their fathers, in that order.

Overall, therefore, the factors affecting outcome for children of absent parents are both complex and frequently controversial. Even the notion of 'absence' itself is not straightforward, as Burghes *et al.* (1997) are at pains to point out:

> The debate about fatherhood frequently treats fathers' physical and psychological presence and absence as synonymous. While fathers who do not live with their children are taken to be in every sense absent from and unavailable to them, resident fathers are assumed to be ever-present and always available. But neither is straightforwardly the case. While it may be more likely and easier for resident fathers to be physically and emotionally available to their children this does not mean that they are always so. Nor are non-resident fathers never present in their children's lives or entirely unavailable to them, even though it may be more difficult for them to be involved. (Burghes *et al.* 1997, p.65)

Fathers absent by reason of imprisonment

Relating the foregoing material in this chapter to fathers who are separated from their children by reason of imprisonment, therefore, a number of factors appear pertinent. First, contact may be more prevalent than imagined, even if it is infrequent or confined to non-face-to-face communication. Second, fathers may be imprisoned, with attendant lowered status and role identity, but still desiring to fulfil their parental role. Third, if there is an established relationship with the children's mother, notably via marriage or other stable relationship, contact may be more likely, as it will if the mother or main carer has a positive regard for the father's parenting abilities. Inimical to continued contact may be paternal violence or abuse, child hostility or developmental change (e.g. adolescence), maternal or extended family influence and geographical distance. The detail of some of these factors, as they affect the parenting role of imprisoned fathers, will unfold in the next section.

Finally, drawing on existing research (e.g. Richards 1989; Schaffer 1990; Wallerstein and Blakeslee 1989), Campion (1995, p.83) sets out six factors worthy of consideration when parents separate. In summary these are:

- the importance to children's well-being of stability and close, affectionate relationships
- the harmfulness of parental conflict as opposed to divorce per se
- the slightly better prognosis of living with the same-sex parent after separation
- no evidence that men's childcare abilities are any less than women's
- better outcomes for children who are able to maintain relationships with both parents
- better adjustment by children whose parents adopt a co-operative and conflict-free approach to their continued parenting.

Again, these are important perspectives which can be applied to children separated from their imprisoned fathers, both during sentence and in preparation for release.

Effects on children

During the early 1990s, some longitudinal research was instituted in the UK looking at the effects upon children and their mothers of imprisonment of the male parent/partner. Richards *et al.* (1994) interviewed 59 fathers (and 65 mothers) from 3 prisons in the south and east of England both 2 months before and 6 months after release. However, they were able to secure these latter interviews only with around half of the men (and two-thirds of the women), thus reducing the representativeness of the findings. Children were not interviewed (this part of the study having been discontinued for practical and ethical reasons) and their perceived reactions were, therefore, represented by their current carers.

A number of findings were of note with respect to the maintenance of father–child relationships. In 11 out of the 26 followed up, men were living in households with some or all of their children. In the majority of other cases, men had some level of contact with their children, most of them fairly regularly. Most of the 26 men reported what they saw as minor problems in their relationships with their children amounting, in the main, to separation anxiety which had manifested itself in 'clinging' and 'following round' behaviour in the early weeks of release, but which had now decreased. This, in a sense, complemented the also largely minor behavioural/emotional problems reported by the children's carers during sentence (e.g. 'cheek', tearfulness, moodiness), most of which the carers attributed to separation from the father and, to an extent, from the disciplinary function he performed.

As in earlier studies (Morris 1965; Shaw 1987) the question of whether or how the children were told of their father's imprisonment was a factor in children's reactions. Most men felt unsupported by professionals. Only 5 of the 26 reported that they had received support (of an advisory nature) from their probation officer after release. Two had approached social services for financial help, one having been refused and the other given a crisis loan. In a series of recommendations, the researchers concluded:

> Carers and partners receive little advice or support. Professional support from the probation services and social services, child counselling and the promotion of self-help groups are needed. (Richards *et al.* 1994, p.118)

This call for a combination of greater professional support and for help with the establishment of self-support systems reiterated the pattern of the US studies cited in Chapter 1 and restated earlier UK recommendations (e.g. Light 1992, 1993; Shaw 1987, 1992). It also led to the setting up in 1990 of the national Federation of Prisoners' Families Support Groups

(FPFSG), which provided a link with some UK studies and publications that followed (e.g. NEPACS 1997; Ramsden 1998).

Another longitudinal investigation of children and their imprisoned fathers during the 1990s was undertaken by Pellegrini (1992, 1997). The emphasis of her research was upon children's own perception of their fathers' incarceration in the context of wider interprofessional, institutional and societal norms and values. Moving beyond Lowenstein's (1986) examination of prisoners' families that identified differential adjustment outcomes according to marital and familial factors, Pellegrini held unstructured interviews with 23 children and their mothers, based upon a juxtaposition of family relationships, development factors and individual perception. Interviews took place in the family home, lasted three to six hours, included researcher observations and were followed up one year later. Basing her theoretical perspective on Magnusson's (1988) interactional approach, proposing that human behaviour is fundamentally meaningful and contextually situated, Pellegrini developed five psychological tasks to be addressed by the children of imprisoned fathers if satisfactory adjustment is to take place:

1. Establishing the meaning of the father's action

2. Acknowledging the separation from the father and adapting daily activities to the new situation

3. Managing feelings elicited by the situation

4. Accepting the father's temporary separation

5. Readjusting to the father's return. (Pellegrini 1997, p.38)

Pellegrini's published accounts do not make entirely clear the structures employed for interpreting her interview data. However, these qualitative data, gathered across the 12-month time span, are drawn upon to suggest that children adopt mechanisms of dissociation in order to incorporate the conflicting images of imprisoned father as 'dad' and imprisoned father as criminal. Thus, a child might find it possible still to retain wholly or partially positive views of the father, by blaming his criminal act on a co-defendant, drugs or alcohol, for example. Pellegrini also argues for the influence of developmental stages, so that primary school children will be more tied to the physical environment and less able to draw upon underlying principles of social norms and values than will adolescents. Thus, dealing with ambivalent feelings towards their fathers may be more problematic for the former than for the latter. This bears out research cited earlier (e.g. Catan *et al*. 1997) about differential developmental responses, as do the findings about the influence of mothers and their explanations on children's images of their fathers (e.g. Arendell 1992, 1995). In respect of this latter:

> The children's mechanisms of dissociation are continuously shaped by their interactions with family members, particularly the mother. Those mothers who have a positive perception of the husband and are optimistic about their future relationship with him are more likely to provide support and consistency to the child's construed mechanism. Conversely, mothers with a negative perception of the husband will make it more difficult for the child to retain the good father image. (Pellegrini 1997, p.40)

In relation to adaptation to the new situation, information tended to leak through slowly to children, via their mothers. Children developed fantasies and anxieties about their fathers which declined after prison visits had reassured them. They tended to keep the knowledge of their father's imprisonment away from their peer group. They also worried about their mother's distress. Fathers with whom there was already a close and sensitive relationship were able to help their children reintegrate their fragmented images and perceptions; those without this level of relationship fared less well. Deep feelings of loss and anger also had to be dealt with by the children; some of the anger was directed at legal authorities, notably the police. Adaptation to the separation was helped where the mother was able to maintain a level of the father's symbolic presence with the family. Children's expectations of their fathers' return home were often disappointed. Commonly things would start off well but swiftly return to old patterns where, for example, the father was out with his friends, drinking a lot, and too busy to spend time with his children.

Despite being small scale, Pellegrini's research is important, partly because it confirmed and updated other related small-scale findings about children's perceptions, and also because it provided important firsthand information from prisoners' children. It also supported findings in the Ormiston Trust study by Noble (1995) who interviewed 30 families in Cambridgeshire, finding that 80 per cent reported behavioural problems in children following their fathers' imprisonment, and a tendency to experience separation from their father as a bereavement, at least in the early stages. This was not helped by traumatic experience of arrest, dawn raids and the like. One-third of the children in Noble's study were reported to have witnessed their fathers' arrest, often accompanied by dogs and several police officers. Wilson (1996), in a review of paternal deprivation by prisoners' children, reiterated the problems to be anticipated at various stages of sentence (i.e. arrest, remand and sentence itself). She compared the process of sudden arrest in the family home to the witnessing of family violence, which has been found to have negative or traumatic effects on children (e.g. Black 1992; Brandon and Lewis 1996). These effects may also be damaging at a stage once removed if, for example, a child suddenly hears of father's arrest at school or via the press.

Where remand is in custody, this period provides different stresses since, as Wilson notes, benefit changes accompany a partner's arrest and mothers are under pressure to make the daily visits allowed to remand prisoners, often under new financial constraints and difficult travelling arrangements, particularly when accompanied by children. McDermott and King (1992) had reported the strain of this situation upon mothers, which was often then passed on to the children. While remand in custody may prepare some families for what is to come, for others, particularly those where men have been remanded on bail, the actual prison sentence may come as a complete shock. Some families may not have known he was in court at all; others may have been led to believe by lawyers, probation officers or the man himself that prison was an unlikely outcome. Noble (1995) found that two-thirds of the mothers/carers in her sample reported deterioration in their children's behaviour (e.g. aggressiveness, anxiety, regression and clinging) at around this time. A small number of these respondents had found support groups helped them to deal with those kinds of problems. A majority (73%), however, were not keen to use support groups and most wanted to avoid the 'stigma' of professional help, preferring to rely on trusted family and friends.

In addition to Noble's (1995) research, the Ormiston Trust was also at around the same time funding an evaluative study of the children's visits scheme at a maximum security prison (Wedge 1995, 1996). This was one of the earliest such schemes to be set up at a men's prison following the Holloway experiment for women (Lloyd 1992b). The scheme, similar to models in other male prisons but with its own characteristics, made provision for visits by children under twelve years to their fathers on one afternoon a week, for up to ten families. The nature and purpose of these visits were explained in the Ormiston Trust's leaflet, available in the prison visitors' centre (including a crèche) also managed by the trust:

> The purpose of children's visits is to enable the inmate to maintain the special relationship he has with his children. To encourage this, Ormiston staff arrange toys, games and activities, board games etc. The inmate is free to move around the room with his children, taking part in any activity they choose. Spontaneous activities are also encouraged, e.g. piggy-back rides.

Wedge (1996) identified four constituents of the experience which had appeared key to the respondents:

- the opportunity for father and child to 'know' one another within a developing and meaningful relationship
- for the father to be able to discharge some parental responsibility within a more involved father–child relationship
- for physical play which confirmed but also moved beyond Lamb's (1981) findings in highlighting the importance of the relationship through play rather than the play itself
- for an increased chance of family survival.

As part of a developing pattern by voluntary and charitable organisations during the 1990s, the Ormiston Trust held conferences for interested parties to discuss the implications of the findings of the studies they had funded. Other agencies' supportive activities included the inception in 1995 of an FPFSG newsletter which later took as its title *Action for Prisoners' Families*, again incorporating an 'awareness into action' emphasis (FPFSG 1998). Also in 1995, Save the Children published a highly comprehensive review of research, policy and practice in relation to prisoners' children (Lloyd 1995). It summarised these aspects of the topic as they applied in the UK and compared them with approaches being taken elsewhere in the world. In particular, it emphasised the legal rights, both of children to go on being parented and of prisoners to continue parenting. Nothing in the research examined suggested that there was any good reason to equate offending behaviour with bad parenting. The review set out Save the Children's stance in relation to children and the prison system:

> Underpinning Save the Children's code of good practice in relation to children and the prison system is the principle that the interests of the child cannot be separated from any decisions made about issuing a custodial sentence to parent or primary carer. A belief in this principle is shared with many individuals and voluntary and statutory agencies who are concerned about the welfare and civil rights of prisoners and their families. Practice at any point of a prisoner's contact with the criminal justice system should reflect this recognition of prisoners' parental responsibilities. (Lloyd 1995, p.11)

Appended to this statement are six underlying principles which can be summarised in terms of:

- the interests of the child being paramount
- minimal disruption to the child during parental imprisonment
- good quality access during imprisonment
- parental responsibilities taken into account
- recognition and co-ordination of support needs of partner/carer
- priority given to the maintenance of the child's established home life.

Partners' views and experiences

In our research, 127 partners/child carers of prisoner fathers were asked about the effects on their children, both at home and at school, of the father being in prison. Only 8 per cent reported no change in their children's behaviour and 22 per cent clearly indicated that behaviour was more difficult. Problems cited included bedwetting, continual questioning by the child, anxiety, withdrawal, violence and the child taking on undue responsibility in the family.

Several respondents also commented that grandparents, especially grandfathers, had become more involved with the children since their fathers went to prison, which had served to help the children. This was clearly a bonus in an otherwise largely negative situation. Of children's behaviour at home, partners told us:

The effect has been enormous. The conviction has resulted in a huge change in circumstances for the family. The press released details of the family so we were harassed by the media. We received threats as the inmate implicated others in the crime. We lost our home and have had to move out of the area. There has been a definite difference in behaviour. The middle child has started to be very aggressive and rude. The youngest child misses Dad greatly and gets very upset. The eldest child feels he can do what he wants now that Dad isn't around. (Children aged 13, 11 and 7)

Very, very affected. It broke their hearts when their dad went away. The offence was reported in the local papers and as we live in a small village it soon became common knowledge. The children [aged 11 and 9] suffered verbal abuse from other children. They were very upset by this and didn't want to go to school. They have been crying a lot and are generally very upset.

Our younger son responds extra warmly to male relatives, especially an uncle. The older son, who was very close to his dad, has had to grow up very fast. He lost a brother two years younger than him when he was six years old; he was very close to this deceased brother so he lost his brother, and now his dad. He finds it very hard to cope. He gets upset and frustrated, and this comes out as anger.

Our daughter [5] was born with [physical defect], and has had several operations for this since her dad has been inside. She has also had a hearing-aid fitted. She has become very clinging over the last few months. [Son, 7] has become very quiet. [Son, 9] has become clinically disturbed, and is seeing a psychiatrist. Last week he shaved his head and made it bleed so that he wouldn't have to go to school the next day, where he is being bullied. Also he has gone to live with my mother and says he won't come home until Daddy comes home. I used to be very extrovert and have become very withdrawn. I've had to move house, to another estate, because the whole family was being bullied, the dog poisoned, the car damaged, the children attacked, etc. There are big financial worries too. Only my sister and one friend support me. The inmate was in the army for 13 years and this is his first time in prison and away from home for any length of time. The children have all been very affected. Why, when the inmate can have home leave now, can't he have it over Christmas when the children desperately want him to be home and can't understand why he can't be? They say they would rather have him there than lots of presents, which he is supposed to be away working in order to buy!

She [daughter of two and a half] gets upset; she is waiting for a major operation. She wants her dad to be there. She keeps asking if Daddy will go to the hospital with her. In fact I have turned down one date because I want him to be there too.

She's been very affected. She has bad asthma and this seems to have got considerably worse since her dad was convicted. I put this down to stress. For the first three or four months our daughter, aged 9, became very argumentative and kept answering back. The effect was worse because we'd not expected her dad to be convicted as it was a first offence. I'd not prepared the child for this so it came as a great shock.

My [foster] daughter was gutted. Her dad had custody of her at the time of the conviction and it meant that she was taken into local authority care. Although her dad was open about the forthcoming trial and the possible consequences, it has been very hard for her. (12-year-old daughter, abandoned by mother, and brought to visits by foster parent)

They've been very affected, especially the one who was Daddy's boy [aged 5]. They couldn't understand at first why he had gone away and were very upset, crying a lot. In the end [inmate] had to tell them why he was away. They were a lot better after that and seemed to settle down.

They have been very affected. I've had difficulty controlling them. They tend to fight a lot and won't do what they're told. I feel that they need a firm father's hand. Because they fight a lot I can't take them anywhere. They play up and behave badly.

Examples were given of a 3-year-old boy whose behaviour had deteriorated significantly since his father went to prison, and who asked for his dad every day, and a 7-year-old boy who had become depressed, was bedwetting and had temper tantrums. Of the latter his mother said:

He has gone back a full year in his schoolwork. The doctor and the school say depression about his dad is the cause.

Partners were, however, generally optimistic about their children's progress at school, with only 5 per cent considering that they were falling behind. Other comments from this minority included the following:

> Son [aged 10] has not been to school since his dad was sentenced. 'I'm not going until Daddy gets out,' he says, and blames everybody for taking [father] away. He was bullied before Dad was sentenced, so he moved school. He still doesn't go – he visits his grandmother or roams the streets. If I try to keep him at home he'll smash things, to get out. He's been referred for counselling. The school has made considerable efforts and so has social services dept. and the education authority psychologists. He is abusive to anyone, violent, deeply disturbed. He has become friendless because of his behaviour. Previously, he was perfectly OK and normal. I'm at my wit's end. (NB A follow-up telephone interview with this mother revealed that, as soon as his father was released, the boy did indeed return to school. When his father was re-arrested, only a fortnight later, the boy resumed his refusal to go to school.)

> Their schooling has been greatly disrupted. The children have had to make new friends and now attend different schools. They got verbal abuse from other children at the old school. The pressure was so great that the children didn't want to go to school.

> [Inmate] was really helpful to [12-year-old] with his homework. I don't have time. I think he has suffered.

Partners/carers were further asked if they had any other comments about imprisoned fathers and their children generally. A few reported that their children were better with father 'away'; most reflected on the dramatic impact of imprisonment on relationships with the children. Respondents' comments that effectively sum up the range of views and experiences of these partners included the following:

> [Child, aged 4] is not sure where she is and wants to know why there are a lot of policemen there. She has only ever known him to be in prison. [Child, aged 12] gets upset and browned off, because he hates the long journeys there and so doesn't always want to visit although he does want to see his dad.

They make it very difficult for men to have contact with their children. It's part of the punishment, separating inmates from their children, but it's the children that suffer the most.

The system's all wrong. There must be better ways of dealing with people who break the law. My partner has lost his business, but he's lucky – he hasn't lost his family. It's a carrot – something to keep him staying clean. Some men lose everything – wife and children. Prison doesn't teach them responsibility. The partners are left with all that. Inmates should be made to be more responsible for their children, with home visits allowed, so that they can do things for their children. They should be allowed to work on licence, so that they can support their families. If everything is taken away, there's no incentive to go straight.

Children growing up without a father is very hard. [Younger son, aged 6] knows no different, but for [older boy aged 12] he has missed out so much. It needs maximum contact to keep families together. It made a difference because they are boys, definitely. There's a strong bond between the boys and their dad.

We [grandparents, who are current carers, and are expecting inmate to take full responsibility for his sons on release] feel that the visiting arrangements do not allow men to focus fully on their children, because there are too many distractions such as other inmates, and it is not macho to be seen to be an active father in front of other prisoners. We would like to see a more 'normal' environment where their dad could practise skills such as cooking for his children, and being with them for longer periods.

I would like the prison system to be more up to date, such as weekend imprisonment with inmates working during the week to support their family and be with them. This would also be less of a burden on the tax payer.

We have adopted a policy of honesty and find it works. [Inmate] has been able to go on being a father by a combination of regular visits, letters, drawings, daily phone calls etc. The Family Visits Day is the best means of doing this – it's long, relaxed, varied, they can have lunch together, and he can play with the children.

Fathers in prison aren't fathers; they are absent fathers. Everyone thinks we have separated and it's true, we have. It's just the same as if we had split up. Of course the children are affected and in my case my daughter has been used to having her father there all the time. Now he's not; it has been devastating for her.

Interviews with prisoners' children

Our study has recorded data on a total of 209 families who, in turn, have the care of 424 children under the age of 18 years. The research had aimed to interview individually around 25 prisoners' children of varying ages, not with any aspiration of gaining a representative view from this large group, but to acquire a sense of some of the feelings and reactions they may experience in relation to their fathers' imprisonment, and to provide a chance for their 'voice' as major players in the subject of this research to be heard.

In the event, although around 25 children were approached, always via their mothers/main carers, 17 were ultimately fully interviewed, the others declining usually by reason of the adult carer's concern for their sensitivity in the situation. A further eight children were part-interviewed in the course of interviews given by their mothers, and are identified via quotes in this section. Twenty-four of the children were identified as of white ethnic majority and one as of black ethnic minority. It was not possible to interview any YOI fathers' children, first because the YOI father sample was small, and second because the average age of YOI fathers' children was less than two years. Before commencing interviews, the researchers always ascertained from the adult carers what understanding the children had of the reason and location surrounding their fathers' absence. In all cases, however, the children had been made fully aware that their fathers were in prison. Ten children from eight families were interviewed in the prison visits waiting area, either before or after their visits to their fathers. It was important to bear in mind that all had travelled a considerable distance, one on public transport, and most had found this tiring. Additionally, six children from two families were visited in their homes and one was interviewed in a café by prior arrangement. With two exceptions (both older teenagers) the children's mothers/carers were present for all or part of the interview.

The ages of the children interviewed ranged from 3 to 19 years (the two 19-year-olds both being under 18 at the time of their fathers' imprisonment). Including the eight part-interviews, all ages within this range were represented at least once. Thirteen children were male and twelve female. Two were stepchildren but this is not referred to when they are quoted since it may identify them and is not material to the point being made. The sample of 17 who were fully interviewed contained 3 who had experienced family visits, 2 who had experienced children's visits and 1 who had experienced a family learning scheme. Of the eight children who were part-interviewed, one had experienced children's visits. The semi-structured interview schedule administered to the 17 child respondents was short, with simple questions, to allow for the wide differences in maturity and understanding within this age range. The interviews began with closed 'warm-up' questions relating to the child's name, age, home area and location of father. More open-ended questions were then posed about the following: likes and dislikes in visiting arrangements; feelings about Dad being away from home; effect of Dad being in prison on life at school; hopes and fears about Dad and family life; the help of letters, photographs, presents/cards, telephone calls, tapes/videos to a continuing relationship with Dad; and any other comment about keeping in touch with Dad. These equated to questions asked of partners/carers about the children's perceptions which, in the eight part-interviews, were put to the children themselves.

It would be invidious to attempt a presentation of these children's views in tabulated form, because of their wide age range and consequent perceptions about their relationships with their fathers and surrounding context. In relation to each open-ended question, therefore, the range of answers is summarised and one or more illustrative quotes provided, ensuring that the complete age range is represented though, inevitably, older children are likely to articulate more fully and fluently than younger ones. Thus, the voices of the children are incorporated in the study as a means of fleshing out and focusing the responses of their parents/carers and leaders of some of the schemes which aim to facilitate and improve their relationships with their fathers. Names and other identifying features have been changed.

Likes and dislikes about visiting Dad

All children interviewed expressed positive feelings about visiting their fathers, but there were mixed views about the visiting arrangements and these clearly varied with the range of facilities available.

Yes, I like visiting my dad and I like playing with other children who come on the visits. Some of them are my friends now. (Jane, aged 5, family learning programme)

Yes, I like it a lot. We play games and I show him my Power Ranger. They searched me. It was funny. (Tom, aged 6, children's visits, part-interview)

I like going to see him. We walk around and play a lot. We can watch the telly and videos too and the prison officers are nice to us. (Shirley, aged 10, family visits, open prison)

There's nothing to do. I get bored. (Sally, aged 3, ordinary visits)

I used to get sad when ordinary visits ended after two hours. I enjoyed family visits when we could be with him all afternoon. But it's much better now that he can visit us at home. (Mike, aged 13, town visits)

Ordinary visits are not long enough. They're too official. He can't be our dad during them. (Sisters aged 11 and 15, ordinary visits, part-interview)

I hated seeing him on ordinary visits at [X] prison. It was a real shock seeing him in prison for the first time. I hated being searched and often had to wait an hour before being called in to see him. The officers were OK though I felt they looked down on me and I could see that some of them were bullies. I didn't like the seating arrangements where he couldn't move. At [Y] prison, the family visits were good, we didn't have to wait long, and the officers were kind and polite and respected you. (Mark, aged 16, town visits)

This prison has a crèche. The one we went to before didn't. I like it in the crèche, but sometimes they don't open it and I get bored. (Julie, aged 8, ordinary visits)

In summary

All like to see Dad; some feel he can't be 'our dad' on visits; most are able to play games with him on visits; smaller ones like to play in crèches and with other children; like TV and videos; bored if no crèche or crèche closed; don't like long waits or short visits; don't like fixed seating arrangements; don't like some prison officers who are portrayed as bullies, but do like others who seem friendly and polite; some don't like being searched, others think it's a game.

Feelings about Dad being in prison

Most children expressed feelings of sadness or distress and commented on the changes (mostly negative) in their lives since their father's imprisonment.

> I was very upset and shocked at first. Over three years I have come to terms with it but I had to develop a 'hard streak' and grow up quickly. Me and my brother have to help Mum a lot with the chores in the house and garden that my dad would normally do. We do it because she needs us to, but I'd rather I hadn't had to. (Mike, aged 13)

> It was difficult at the beginning, really difficult. I felt so angry with him for doing it – and confused. Mum and Dad have both been very open about what happened [fraud] and that's helped. It's better to talk about it. (Paula, aged 19, part-interview)

> When he was at home there was lots of tension in the house. Dad was emotionally up and down. At 7.00 am one morning there was a knock on the door. The police had come to arrest Dad and search the house. Within minutes my mother was saying, 'That's it. I want a divorce.' He stayed in the house from charge to sentence and life was hell for everyone. Now he's in prison, he and my Mum have split up. But it's actually reduced the tension and life is really much easier now. I only realised two months after he'd gone what a nightmare it had been. If you live with something long enough you get used to it. He's my dad though, and I love him anyway and always will. (Jim, aged 19)

> Dad is in prison because he has been naughty. But when we come to see him, he can play with us and buy us drinks and crisps. (Brothers aged 5 and 6, part-interview)

I feel sad. My Mum does the shouting now. My dad used to do it. (Jane, aged 5)

I used to spend lots of time with Dad, so I see him a lot less now. I don't speak to him so much. I miss that. (Sue, aged 11, part-interview)

When he first went to prison I really missed him and used to cry a lot in bed at night. I didn't want my mum to know I cried because that would have just upset her too. But now I spend a lot of time with my friends and sometimes I don't visit him if I'm doing other things. Mum thinks I should but when he rings up he tells me he understands and not to worry about it. (Jenny, aged 14)

In summary

Children become upset, angry, shocked, sad, confused; miss seeing and speaking to him; honest talking helps; home is less tense now; children had to grow up quickly and help Mum more at home; children protecting Mum from own distress; teenage friendships sometimes take precedence; Mum does shouting now, where Dad used to do it.

Effect on life at school

Not surprisingly, school was a key factor in most of these children's lives. They all had to deal in some way with their father's imprisonment in respect of this setting.

I told all my friends. They've been great, very supportive. (Paula, aged 19, part-interview)

At my previous school, I had a friend whose dad was in prison and we used to talk quite a lot about how it felt [upsetting and annoying] and this was a big support. Now I've moved to this school, I've just told one or two people I trust and I think they've kept my secret. (Mike, aged 13)

Some children take the mick. They say, 'Your dad's never going to come out.' (David, aged 9)

The school has been helpful and supportive and got me out of trouble sometimes when I bunked off. Some people at school discovered my dad was in prison and they gossiped for a couple of months. It's getting better now. (Mark, aged 16)

Since he went away, finances have been difficult. There was less money around to buy me the things other kids had. (Carl, aged 18, part-interview)

I know my Dad's been naughty so that's why we come here. But my friends think he's at work. Some are nasty to me but not because of him. (Mandy, aged 4)

They bully me, say nasty things. I don't let them know I care, but sometimes I cry on the way home. The teachers don't know my dad's in prison and I don't want to tell them. (Alan, aged 7)

I really miss him taking me to school. That was when we used to talk. The head and two of my teachers have been really good, though. I felt embarrassed about it at first but they have made it easy for me to talk to them. (Jemma, aged 17)

School helps me forget. (Luke, aged 12)

In summary

School helps children to forget; some people gossip; some people support; less money to buy things other kids have; some bullying, gossiping, saying nasty things; some teachers know; some teachers don't know; children missing Dad taking them to school.

Hopes and fears about Dad and family life

Most children entertained a mixture of hopes and fears for their continuing and future relationships with their fathers.

Hopes

Our oldest brother had to go into care a few years ago. We all want him back. We want our dad back with us too so we can all be a family again. (Siblings, aged 6 and 9)

Just to have him home with us on [inmate's earliest parole date]. I want to help him with his work and for him to teach me to drive. (Mike, aged 13)

I hope he'll get his act together and find work and accommodation on release. (Jim, aged 19)

I feel I've now got myself together – no drugs, good friends, a job, enough money. But my dad is very strict. There'll need to be some adjustment when he comes out. (Mark, aged 16)

That he gets through all right. (Jemma, aged 17)

I want his sentence to be over [he's out in two months' time] and just have life and our family back to normal. I hope nothing like this will ever happen again – and I don't think it will. (Hindpal, aged 14)

I want him to come home. (Mandy, aged 4)

Fears

He won't come home. (Mandy, aged 4)

I was worried he'd change once he went to prison but it's not so. He's still protective and concerned for us and rings to check we've arrived home safely after a visit. (Jenny, aged 14)

That we'll never be the original family unit again. I worry that Dad will drift on release. He's not very inclined to get up and do things. He might get back in with the wrong crowd again. (Jim, aged 19)

I felt abandoned when he came here. I still do and I don't feel sure that he'll come home to us even when he gets out, though he says he will. (Luke, aged 12)

That he won't be able to find a job and we'll go on living without enough money. (Jemma, aged 17)

He'll come out and do it again and maybe it'll be my fault because he thinks he has to make a lot of money to buy things for me. (Carl, aged 18, part-interview)

I've no fears really. I don't think he'll do it again. He's learnt his lesson from this. (Mike, aged 13)

Hopes surrounded Dad surviving the sentence, Dad coming home, the family being reunited, Dad being able to adjust, Dad finding work and accommodation if he can't go home, mutual help between Dad and child.

Fears ranged from none to those concerning Dad not coming home, changing during sentence, realising children's fears of abandonment, poverty, reinforcing associated guilt, Dad drifting, reoffending.

The help of other types of contact to the child–father relationship

While visits are a major way of continuing father–child contact, other non-face-to-face means of contact also serve the important purpose of reminding children that their absent father continues to think of them between visits.

Letters

All children like receiving and sending letters.

> We don't send them now because he comes home on town visits. But at the last prison we wrote weekly and I've kept all his letters. They really helped me. (Mark, aged 16)

> He likes to get my drawings and he sends me some back with funny faces on. (Tom, aged 6, part-interview)

Photographs

Again all children liked to look at photographs of their fathers and knew that their fathers in turn kept photographs of them. Some of those who attended certain children's or family visits schemes had also had family photographs taken on the visit.

> I've got a photo of me with my sister, my mum and my dad when we went on a family visit. They took it on a polaroid camera so we could see it straight away, and they took another one for my Dad. I look at it every day and I think about when we'll all be together again. (Shirley, aged 10)

The photos at home with Dad on were taken over three years ago. We've sent him some new ones but they upset him because he wasn't there at Christmas when we took them. Looking at the old ones of him I feel sad because things were happy then, but at least I know he's still the same person and he still loves us even though he's away from us. (Luke, aged 12)

Presents and cards

These were again a universally appreciated medium of contact, though the facility was variable in nature.

He sent me a birthday card with a big red flower on. It was nice. But he's not allowed to send presents. My mum buys me a present from both of them. (Julie, aged 8)

When we went in on the family visit Dad gave me a present of a teapot and my sister got a chinese tea set. We can take things in for him too and he likes it. (Diane, aged 6)

Telephone calls

This was a very important means of contact for all children.

He rings us four or five times a day from this prison. It's good. We're always talking to him and he tells us to be good for Mum. (David, aged 9)

He does phone us three or four nights a week but there's usually only time for him to talk to Mum and I wish I could have a call just to myself. I worry about what it costs him though. (Jenny, aged 14)

Tapes and videos

A minority of adult respondents in the study referred to their children playing tapes with their dad on (and indeed a specific scheme to encourage this practice is described in Chapter 4). However, only one of the children interviewed had a videotape on which he could both see and hear his father and thus be reminded of him.

I play it quite often. Sometimes it helps me forget that he's not with us any more. So when it's playing I'm happy but when it's finished, I'm gutted. (Carl, aged 18, part-interview)

Other comments from children

Other comments came from 6 of the 17 children, who provided complete interviews, when asked if there was anything else they would like to say about keeping in touch with their fathers.

We have a good relationship. I'll take the future as it comes. It'll be OK when Dad comes out. (Mark, aged 16)

There are degrees of crime. Murder or sexual crime might have been harder for me to come to terms with. But for my brother, it's all or nothing – Dad's now a criminal. He's very anti-Dad. (Jim, aged 19)

More phone calls should be allowed and he should get weekend leave. (Sue, aged 11)

One day I was nearly abducted by a man in a black van. My mum and my sisters and brothers were really upset. The next day my dad came home to see me with some prison officers. He was one beautiful dad. (David, aged 9)

My mum and dad have always been honest with me about what has happened and I'd rather have that than them lying to me, telling me he was working away or something. It's been hard and sometimes my brother and I can talk about it but other times he just stays quiet and keeps it all inside. I think I'm better at talking about it. (Mike, aged 13)

I'm sad that he's in prison. I was happy when he came out before and sad when he went back in again. (Jane, aged 5)

In summary

These children are expressing a wide range of emotions and attitudes from sadness, to judgement of the crime, philosophical acceptance, wanting more contact, needing Dad around when one of them was in danger, needing to talk and finally appreciating parental honesty.

Taking these quotations overall, it is clearly difficult to put children's responses into neat categories. They differ in age, sex, family, school and life experiences and developmental stages. Some are old enough to have formed judgements of their fathers' behaviour and are dealing with the accompanying tensions, while younger children remain preoccupied with the emotions they feel for their absent parent. It nevertheless remains apparent that none of them is untouched by the loss of their father to imprisonment. All would prefer not to be in the situation in which they find themselves. Many, for example, are affected within the school setting, to a degree which was underestimated by their parents. Most appreciate any possible opportunity for contact and would like to have more if it were available. Although there are sometimes related fears, all are looking forward to the day when their fathers will return home and, where this is a possibility, they will become a whole family once again.

The findings reported above reflect and expand upon some of the earlier studies cited in the chapter in respect of child and family privations during paternal imprisonment. Some of the children's responses are reminiscent of Pellegrini's (1997) findings about children's mechanisms for incorporating conflicting images of their fathers. Nevertheless, most of the children interviewed for the present study appeared to have close and sensitive relationships with their fathers which, according to Pellegrini, are significant in helping them reintegrate their fragmented images and perceptions. Children who do not have psychologically and physically supported access to their imprisoned fathers may therefore, perhaps, fare less well and are in particular need of assistance from schools and the caring professions to enable them to express their feelings, with the aim of reducing negative and damaging effects for the future.

CHAPTER FOUR

Provision for Father–Child Contact

The facilities which afford prisoners potential contact with their children vary between establishments. All prisons have an ordinary visits system, while one in twelve of adult prisons runs special children's visits or family visits schemes. All prisons also permit the exchange of letters and outgoing telephone calls. Some prisons allow the exchange of audiotapes between inmates and children. While some of these contact arrangements tend to operate in a fairly similar manner across establishments, they are all subject to the discretion of the individual prison governor.

In order that the main substance of the present research data can be placed in its statutory and policy contexts, it is appropriate here to provide an account of the different types of visits, and other contacts involving their children, which prisoners may make and receive. The account will include views from staff about children's and family visits, and comments from inmates and partners about the usefulness of non-face-to-face means of contact between children and fathers. The logistics for families in terms of travelling to and from prisons will also be described.

Ordinary visits

In its discussion of literature and issues relating to imprisoned fathers, Chapter 1 made reference to Prison Service Standing Order no. 5 as it obtained prior to June 1997 when Section 5 of the Standing Orders relating to communications was consolidated. The change contained inclusive language and added security considerations, all of which are italicised:

It is one of the roles of the Prison Service to ensure that the socially harmful effects of an inmate's removal from normal life are as far as possible minimised, and that contacts with the outside world are maintained. Outside contacts are therefore encouraged, especially between an inmate and his *or her* family and friends. *At the same time, the Prison Service has an overriding duty to hold inmates in lawful custody in well ordered establishments; and to have regard to the prevention of crime and similar considerations; and some regulation of inmates' communications is therefore necessary.*

This 'consolidation' process (which, effectively, amended Circular Instruction 11/1991 concerning visits to inmates) covered conditions in respect of visits (Section A), correspondence (Section B) and telephone calls (Section G). They are the conditions that apply to prisoner/family communications at the time of writing. Following a comprehensive survey of the prison estate, however, a review of visiting provisions is taking place, under the auspices of the Prisoner Communications and Family Ties Section of the Prison Service Agency, which will report in three phases. The first phase, due to be completed during 2001, will report on contemporary problems such as the process of booking visits, eligibility for accumulated visits and drug smuggling during visits. Phase two will review arrangements for legal and official visits. Phase three will report on administrative procedures, including the use of modern technology such as closed circuit TV during visits.

In addition to this, a new Prison Service Order (no. 4400) was issued in July 1998, with the title 'Child Protection Measures'. This sets out mandatory action to minimise risks which paedophile prisoners in particular may pose to children via visits, phone calls or letters. This action, for example, requires governors to ensure that names and ages of all visiting children are included on visiting orders and that convicted paedophiles may only receive visits from their own children and siblings. Their correspondence and phone calls are also likely to be closely monitored under this order. The combination of this new order and the consolidation and review processes therefore reflect an ever-growing concern with security provisions which, though necessary and understandable, inevitably impinge quite significantly upon the ethos of trying to maintain 'normal' family relationships, expressed in the first part of Standing Order no. 5.

Convicted prison inmates are entitled to two visits within a four-week period, though visits should be allowed as frequently as circumstances permit. (Incentive schemes allow some prisoners to have extra or 'enhanced' visits.) At least one of these visits should be on a Saturday or Sunday if the inmate wishes. The minimum length of visit is 30 minutes, but should normally be at least one hour and in practice is often two. These arrangements also apply to unconvicted inmates who may, however, have visits on at least three days per week.

To gain entry to a prison, visitors and accompanying children must be in possession of a valid visiting order, on which they are named. This will have been initiated by the inmate. Up to three persons (excluding children under ten years) are normally allowed at each visit. They will wait till their name is called for the visit, either in a visits waiting area or in one of the many prison visitors centres, which are usually run by volunteers or paid members of charitable organisations. Here they may be able to obtain refreshments if they choose and many centres contain supervised crèches for younger children. At some point prior to entering the visits room adult visitors and, increasingly, their children will be searched by prison officers to ensure that no unauthorised articles, notably drugs, are passed between a visitor and an inmate. In practice, a search normally comprises the emptying of handbags into trays and the retention of tablets or sharp objects such as scissors or penknives. Visitors also pass through a body scanner both before and after visits.

The consolidated rules on visits state that they should take place under the most humane conditions possible subject to security considerations. In respect of the latter, therefore, an inmate found taking drugs would be likely to be placed on closed visits, which often occur in a visiting box with a screen window separating inmate and visitors, so that physical contact is prevented. Normal visits, however, should be held in open visiting rooms with both inmate and visitors seated at a table, and inmate and visitors should be permitted to embrace each other. Some visits rooms contain crèches or children's play areas, some of which are supervised and others not. There is a refreshment facility in most visiting halls and in some prisons the prisoner is allowed to go and purchase refreshments for his visitors, in the process perhaps being able to take his children along too and buy them a drink and a bar of chocolate, for example. In other prisons, again because of security considerations, the opportunity for this 'normalising' behaviour is being reduced via a system of fixed tables and chairs from which the prisoner is not allowed to move. One of these systems, known as 'the snake', consists of one long fixed table in the shape of a curved snake, the height of which is sometimes such that children cannot see over it. Again, increasingly, prison staff play a surveillance role which requires them to observe whether articles have been passed or whether conversations or behaviour suggest illegality or risk to others.

Although arrangements for all visits are at the discretion of individual prison governors, the review process referred to earlier aims to standardise these procedures across the prison estate. These arrangements include 'special' visits, one-off visits arranged with a specific purpose, often to resolve a family crisis, with a probation officer or chaplain in attendance. They also include extended visiting schemes such as children's visits, family visits and family learning schemes, for example, which are available to certain prisoners at some but not all prisons.

Children's and family visits

Children's and family visits schemes were set up in men's prisons during the 1990s, largely as a response to the success of a parallel experiment for imprisoned mothers and their children at HMP Holloway (Lloyd 1992b). There has been no previous research of this group of schemes. The present survey identified 11 such arrangements operating in adult male prisons at the end of 1996, and 8 by the end of 1998, 3 of them having been suspended because of drug conveyance during the research period. There was, therefore, a point during the research period at which all existing schemes were being studied for this project. None of these was running at private prisons or at YOI establishments though, since the research finished, four YOI establishments have adopted such provision.

Although the researchers made arrangements to visit institutions responsible for eight schemes, one of them had been suspended by the time of the visit because of drug smuggling and has not resumed (though some of its previous users were interviewed). Another one had been similarly suspended but did resume. Two others were in abeyance because of building works but did resume towards the end of the research period, partly accounting for a group rather than an individual interview of partners/carers in one establishment. A further prison which had operated a family visits scheme, where partners and children could come in and make use of the prison swimming pool and gymnasium as a family, had originally been earmarked for study but had to be abandoned because its scheme was also suspended due to the passing of drugs and 'indecent' behaviour by some of the adults. As a consequence, the prison chaplaincy was doing what it could to facilitate and staff one-off family visits in the chaplaincy where 'a special need' had been identified.

The purpose in detailing these changes is to highlight the considerable volatility in the provision of special visits schemes, with the overall trend in the adult estate appearing to be one of closure rather than expansion. This is in contrast to that of parenthood courses, which have been shown to be on the increase, but which of course do not normally involve access to visitors and the accompanying security risk. Although these visiting schemes represent variations on a single ethos surrounding quality time for prisoners and their families, with a particular emphasis on relationships between fathers and children, there is some diversity in their length, frequency, content and eligibility criteria. This again reflects the fact that they operate at the discretion of individual prison governors and need to fit in with the other systems and constraints of the particular prison.

Five of the prisons studied ran schemes known as children's visits, two a scheme known as family visits and one a scheme called the family learning programme. Length of children's visits varied from one hour in a closed local prison to five and a quarter hours, including lunch, in a closed training prison. Two took place weekly, one fortnightly, one monthly, and one bi-monthly. Only one scheme operated at a weekend. Two were for fathers and children only, so that children could have the undistracted attention of their fathers. The rest included the accompanying adult(s). Toys, games, writing and drawing materials and a space for playing physical games were commonly available. Visits were limited to a maximum number of families, averaging around ten. Child-care staff and volunteers were usually on hand and surveillance by uniformed staff kept to a minimum; in at least one case a senior prison officer and prison officer gave time voluntarily to the co-ordination of the scheme. Child eligibility ranged from under 12 to under 15 years; prisoner eligibility was being a father, stepfather (or in two cases a grandfather) with no record of drug use in prison. Men were usually screened in some way, for example in one case by applying to the prison probation officer who assessed their suitability.

Some had to have served a minimum length of sentence, normally between one and six months. All these visits were additional to the normal visits entitlement and all were expected to focus upon the children.

The two family visits schemes operated in a closed training prison and an open prison respectively, the former weekly for five and a quarter hours, the latter on eight days a year for six hours. The first was primarily for inmates serving four years and over, the second for inmates reaching the end of what were usually sentences in excess of five years. Again, a record of prison drug use would exclude inmates from this facility. Both allowed up to six visitors, including children of any age; both made lunch available to families. At the open prison, barbecues could be had during the summer months, and at other times the prisoner himself could cook the family's lunch. In the case of family visits there was usually some element of voluntary agency staffing and again minimal prison officer surveillance. The focus of this kind of visit is to strengthen family ties and inmates are again encouraged to participate in play and activities with their children.

The family learning programme, versions of which have begun to spread to a small number of other prisons including one YOI since this study commenced, is a 15-week programme of literacy support for prisoners, partners and their children. It is run by the education department within a prison and constitutes a weekly two-hour weekday visit for between five and six families who are helped by adult basic skills tutors and a crèche worker to encourage their children to read, write, draw, develop numeracy skills, and so on. The overall aim is to improve care and rehabilitation for prisoners through promoting their ongoing involvement with their children's development and education via a family learning endeavour. To be eligible, prisoners must have preschool children and be without a record of drug use within the prison.

Ten staff (all of white ethnic majority) from the eight schemes outlined above were interviewed and relevant documentation obtained. Via a scheduled interview questionnaire, they were asked about the structure, purpose, advantages/disadvantages and evaluation/outcome of the schemes. Clearly variations across these schemes preclude the possibility of a homogeneous response from staff members, but identifiable issues emerged and these are outlined below.

Reasons/thinking behind the schemes

Most of these visits schemes have been in existence for at least three years, some for as long as six but, as explained above, some have been interrupted for security reasons. The thinking behind them has universally been to further positive relations between prisoner fathers and their children through the provision of an additional facility for this purpose. An examination of the documentation surrounding these schemes tends to reveal the dual long-term aims of prisoner rehabilitation via the strengthening of family ties and the serving of the best interests of the child through the provision of good quality access to the imprisoned father. As is also the case with parenthood courses, the longevity of these schemes is frequently the result of the enduring commitment of their leaders who also act as 'product champions'.

Programme leaders

Of the eight schemes included in the study, all involved uniformed staff in some capacity, but this was usually minimal, suggesting sensitivity to family privacy and also a relaxation of security, partly because of smaller numbers of visitors and partly because of prisoner screening. Most children's and family visits had significant involvement from charitable trusts and/or volunteer workers. The family learning scheme was led by the education department co-ordinator, an adult basic skills tutor and a crèche worker.

Programme length and continuation

As outlined above, the longest running of the schemes was six years and the shortest (the literacy programme) three years. All staff who ran these facilities were extremely enthusiastic about them, pointing out their advantages to both prisoner and child. Again, the continuation of these projects rested significantly upon the commitment of these staff. As has already been shown, however, the projects were liable to be suspended or stopped completely if any participants behaved inappropriately, notably by passing drugs. Additionally, all were dependent to a greater or lesser degree upon outside funding. Although prison-based personnel could carry on running them if this funding (and accompanying extra staffing) were removed, it was unlikely that, as non-essential facilities, they would be prioritised for continuation. As an example, one scheme had initially run two parallel family cohorts and had a long waiting list for entry, but one cohort had to fold because of lack of available prison staff. Despite these uncertainties, however, at the time of study all schemes were expected to continue for the foreseeable future.

Scheme funding

All children's and family visits schemes had some form of staffing assistance from voluntary or charitable bodies such as, for example, NEPACS (North Eastern Prisoner After Care Society) and the Ormiston Children and Families Trust. The family learning programme was funded initially through a grant from the basic skills agency and subsequently from the general purpose fund which provides for programme equipment. The local county library service provided a stock of books and the cost of children's tables and chairs came from prison funds. While, as suggested above, all schemes visited for the study were expected to continue, the history of one children's visits scheme is that the involved charitable body withdrew its funding because of low take-up and, as a consequence, the facility ceased to exist. Although it has subsequently been reinstated and funds restored, it is a reminder of the fragility of such schemes and the fact that prison-based support alone is unlikely to be sufficiently substantial to ensure durability.

Organisation of schemes

All prisoner fathers participated in these schemes voluntarily, as did their partners and children, though clearly children's involvement stemmed from parental guidance and preference. Inmate entry was contingent upon eligibility and was also to some extent a consequence of the sentence planning process, where personal officers had advised fathers of the availability and suitability for them of such a scheme. Another material factor was the extent to which the scheme had been publicised within the prison. All schemes had some form of poster and/or publicity leaflets, but scheme leaders did not always have control over the extent to which they were distributed across the establishment concerned. Two leaders, however, had arranged to go to speak periodically to groups of men on the wings about the existence and purpose of the schemes. At least two also saw the men prior to the visits to ensure they understood that the emphasis of the scheme was upon the needs of the children to have attention, conversation and play with their fathers. Apart from the family learning programme, which being educative had high staff input, most other visits schemes allowed families or father–children groupings to choose how to spend their time together. However, a combination of volunteers and staff co-ordinators was invariably on hand to guide fathers' attention to toys, games and other joint activities which could be drawn upon as an important part of family interaction. They would also proactively assist, for example, in the crèche, where requested.

All staff referred to the importance of continuing liaison with prison personnel in order to overcome suspicion and security problems. In the words of one scheme co-ordinator:

> It took us 18 months of planning and security hurdles, doubts and suspicions from other staff, including the POA [Prison Officers Association] before we could get the scheme off the ground. But the vast majority are now in favour, having seen it up and running.

As this comment suggests, most staff felt that not only were they responsible for providing a facility for fathers and families, but also for demonstrating they could do so efficiently, effectively and with minimal threat to the security considerations uppermost in the minds of prison staff.

Advantages of children's and family visits schemes

These comments from involved staff members sum up all the advantages referred to in the survey:

> This scheme allows men to relate to their families. It's actually 'hands on', unlike the ordinary visits set-up. For some, it's their first experience of getting down and playing with their kids. (Charitable trust co-ordinator, family visits)

> Here, the children get individual quality time with parents but it's child-focused time. It helps maintain relationships between parents, which the children need to see. It provides emotional and practical support from fathers to mothers and the children can watch this and

learn by example. We had a case of a child who was on the verge of being excluded from school for difficult behaviour. The headteacher rang me and we were able to admit the child and his parents to the programme. His mum and dad actually played with this child for the first time. Previously they had both been too busy working. The result was that the child then settled down at school and was able to remain there. (Education co-ordinator, family learning programme)

I'm a dad myself, so watching these children's faces as they play with their dads makes me quite emotional. The ones who come regularly look really excited and run over to their dads when they arrive, whereas some of them were hesitant to start with. It changes the men too, there's no doubt about that. You've got to believe there's hope for these families for the future though some staff are cynical about that. We also have to make security a priority but we try to search partners and children respectfully. (Prison officer, children's visits)

The above comments highlight the importance for each member of the family and for the child in particular of having a positive, child-centred, interactive family experience. They also show the changes that can take place over a period of time, in respect of both men and their children, again emphasising the dual benefits of prisoner rehabilitation within the family and the quality of children's contact with their absent father.

Disadvantages of children's and family visits schemes

The drawbacks of these schemes are again summarised below in the words of involved staff members.

Those who are actually involved in the scheme really get a lot out of it. The problems are mainly practical – getting it publicised in the prison, travelling to get here quite early in the morning and the cost of the extra visits for partners. (Visits centre co-ordinator, family visits)

The goodbyes can be very painful. As a parent myself, I find it very upsetting when children get distressed leaving the visit. For example, we had a 5-year-old child today who became hysterical, crying, screaming and clinging to her father. (Prison officer, children's visits)

We've had no negative feedback ever, except on the length of the morning and the length of the programme – i.e. they want more! (Tutor, family learning programme)

The foregoing comments indicate no real disadvantage in the content of any of these schemes. However, there are some practical difficulties, particularly for families, with cost and time of travelling and with getting the schemes publicised. The schemes are popular and participants want more, but resources do not allow this. Finally, the downside for children of emotional reunion with their fathers is the renewed experience of separation and this can be difficult for all concerned.

Scheme evaluation

Only one scheme had previously been externally evaluated and positively so (Wedge 1995), although another had been described in a prison newsletter and several had been the subject of conference discussions (e.g. NEPACS 1997). Only the family learning programme made use of internal monitoring forms (as well as weekly diaries for parents) at the time of the study. In this one case, parents evaluated jointly in the spirit of the overall family learning exercise and, as the quote above suggests, feedback was always positive. As all the foregoing information indicates, staff feedback to researchers in respect of the present study was also extremely positive.

When asked about plans for evaluation, all felt that this would be a desirable development, particularly as many were aware of the need to prove to governors and external funders that their schemes were effective in relation to their overall aims. However, there seemed little likelihood of this key development without the funds to pay external evaluators who could offer both credibility and objectivity in this situation. Not unrelated, as a range of other staff comments showed, there was some way to go in resolving the mistrust of some prison staff about the existence of these schemes.

Other staff comments

We know we have to go on being careful about security, though suspicions that the programme would enable drugs to be brought in have never been founded so far. We have to be careful about equipment – e.g. playdough could make key moulds; scissors and pencil sharpeners could become weapons. (Education co-ordinator, family learning programme)

The normality for families of being together for a whole day, eating lunch together, walking round the grounds, kicking a football around, is something very rare in the prison system. Most men have served a lot of years and waited a long time to get to this point. You can't help feeling that this kind of thing should have been available to the children throughout. But the fact is that the men have shown that they are villains and they have a lot to prove before the prison authorities are going to trust them in this way. (Prison officer, family visits, open prison)

It's become a smooth operation now. But dedicated uniformed staff volunteers are hard to find. If the current ones move on, who knows what will happen? A substantial number of uniformed staff are (or act as if they are) anti-prisoners and family. Volunteering is very hard for ranked officers. (Probation officer, children's visits)

These comments highlight the overriding concern for security issues, about which all staff are extremely conscious. They also demonstrate the crucial need for involvement of uniformed staff who are in sympathy with the ethos of the child's welfare in the shape of continuing child–father relationships during imprisonment.

Travelling to visits

We were conscious that for many of those making visits of any kind to inmates in prison the journey can be particularly difficult. About half of the partners (47%) told us that their journey was either 'very easy' or 'quite easy' whether they came by car or public transport. By contrast, 45 per cent told us that their journeys were not easy because they lived at a distance and either the car journey was long or public transport was difficult, and often visiting was an expensive business. Some families made extraordinary efforts to visit regularly and to maintain father–child contact, often in the face of considerable difficulty.

It's very hard. Three hundred and eighty miles round trip. Costs around £50 each time.

It's very difficult; we have to travel by train and the journey takes seven hours, all for a two-hour visit. I can't get any help with travelling expenses as the child has her mother's surname on the birth certificate.

It's difficult. The journey takes three hours each way on public transport and is also very expensive. The day costs between £15 and £20. I'm on benefits so can't really afford to come.

It's very difficult. I don't drive and have to rely on other people to bring me. Today I travelled by taxis as I could not get a lift and it cost me £100. I had to come because if I had failed to turn up, my partner would not have been able to book another family visit for three months and it would have been a further two months before the visit itself. My friends have recently let me down over lifts because they have grown tired of the commitment.

It's a difficult journey, especially with a small child. We have to change trains twice and it's very expensive as the only way to get from the station to the prison is by taxi and each visit costs £25.40 in travel expenses. I cannot claim for these as I'm not the inmate's wife and the child is not the inmate's natural child or adopted. (Child is a stepson)

I bring three children on public transport: daughter of 4, son of 2 [in pushchair] and daughter 3 months [in baby sling].

As I have difficulties managing and travelling with our six children, I rotate visits, bringing three children each time. (The children are aged 13, 11, 9, 7, 2 and 6 months)

In the light of such comments, it was no surprise that a third of partners (with their children) told us that they had sometimes been prevented from coming to visit the inmate by the difficulties posed by travelling arrangements.

Yes. Having no transport and not being able to afford to come. I get no assistance with the costs of travel. Sometimes the organising is just too difficult; for example, I can't find anyone to look after the three children I leave at home when I take the other three on a visit.

Yes. He has about 30 unused visiting orders because we couldn't get there. Also we need to raise cash upfront for journeys, and it's not refunded until claimed [with proof of travel] later.

Yes. I have been let down with lifts and that was very disappointing. His probation officer said he would take me too but he let me down as well. I would like to come more often, but it's so expensive.

Yes, I would like to come every week but I have to find the money out of the weekly budget so that makes it very difficult to manage.

No. I'd come rain or shine, even though I can't afford it. I have to take the travel costs out of the food money.

Town visits

Prisoners in the later stages of sentence may, under incentives and earned privileges schemes, be deemed eligible for day release at a weekend, during which time they may travel within a given radius of the prison. Most prisoners use this privilege to meet with their families and spend the day with them. Town visits can take place on anything between a weekly and monthly basis according to the individual patterns of the prison.

Home leave

Following a review in 1995, home leave, as it is still commonly known, was replaced by release on resettlement licence. Together with release on compassionate licence (usually for a prisoner who is his child/children's primary carer and needs release to ensure the continuing welfare arrangements for his child/children), this takes place via temporary release arrangements under Instructions to Governors 36/1995. All such arrangements are privileges, under Prison Rule 6, for which prisoners must apply and are subject to a full risk assessment (i.e. one which assesses risks to public safety, further offending, non-compliance, absconding, suitability of overnight accommodation, if applicable, and acceptability to the public). Prisoners serving between one- and four-year sentences become eligible to apply for home leave after serving one-third of those sentences including remand periods; the eligibility of those serving over four years is contingent upon their parole eligibility date. Home leave commonly takes the form of a long weekend at the prisoner's home address, with conditions for reporting to the local probation office.

Non-face-to-face contact

While visits are clearly a significant means of maintaining family relationships, communication may be further sustained and enhanced by non-face-to-face methods in the interim or, on occasion, in place of visits. Most frequently, the methods comprise correspondence and telephoning; less frequently, they also include tape-recording.

Letters and cards

Section B of the consolidated Prison Standing Orders encourages inmates to 'keep in touch with the outside world through letter writing' and emphasises that privacy of correspondence should be respected as far as possible. Levels of censorship vary from one prison establishment to another, but have in general relaxed in recent years. All convicted prisoners are allowed to send one 'statutory' letter (i.e. a letter at public expense) per week and may purchase one or more further 'privilege' letters with their own monies. A statutory letter may also be sent in place of a statutory visit.

Further to this, a 'special' letter may be sent in specific circumstances, for example, to a lawyer or probation officer, or occasionally for family welfare reasons. Unconvicted inmates may send two statutory letters per week and as many further privilege letters as they wish. The permitted length of letters is at the governor's discretion but at least four sides of A5 paper must be made available. If cards are obtainable in the prison canteen, these may be purchased and sent within the letter entitlement, and up to 12 Christmas cards (more at some establishments) may also be purchased and sent. At prisons where correspondence is not normally censored, there is no restriction on the number or length of letters which inmates may receive. Where censorship exists, inmates can receive as many letters as they send out. By this means, therefore, imprisoned fathers may have either one-way or reciprocal contact with their children.

The previous chapter demonstrated children's pleasure in any kind of contact with their fathers, including letters. The majority of partners also considered every kind of contact to be of benefit. This was supported by the group respondents who said that all contacts help to keep the father–child relationship 'alive'. In our study, although just over a third of those adults and a half of young offenders responding with information exchanged no correspondence at all with their child/children, almost half of adults and young offender respondents reported a frequency of at least once a week.

The frequency of letters allowed to inmates varies across prisons and to some extent the above figures will reflect this. Making allowance for this and possible literacy problems, the amount of correspondence between family and inmate is arguably relatively high. Certainly its importance should not be underestimated. For example, one inmate said:

> They all stand in a line when they get their three letters from me. I might have said 'Are you being a good girl?' and they will reply 'I am Dad'. It makes them each feel a bit special. They realise they can keep in touch by writing and drawing and tell me how they are getting on.

Partners made the following comments:

> There are lots of letters between all of them. He always puts on them 'Be home soon'. That helps them because their own father just walked out one night and it reassures them that he's thinking about coming back. (Inmate is their stepfather)

> Even though he is not around, he is involved in everything they do. They write regularly; he likes to see their progress in writing. He's allowed to have photos taken on children's visits and these are put up in the bedroom. There is reciprocal celebration of important events. He phones every night because it helps him to stay involved; they tell him all their doings. There are videos with Dad which are played to remind us of happy times. Also the eldest boy plays videos of his dad's favourite films to keep himself in touch with Dad.

> Letters just remind them of him and that he cares for them. [Four year old] likes to draw things for her dad and to talk about him. She tells everyone at school he's working away.

> Contact includes pictures or paintings and [the inmate's] walls are covered with them. [Our daughter aged 3] now gives an order of the drawings she would like from her father. This has helped him build up a strong relationship which is especially important as he only sees her four times a year. (Parents are estranged and inmate's ex-partner and their child live at a great distance from the prison. Mother has recorded the child talking and singing on audiotape.)

Presents and cards

Similarly, about two-thirds of adult inmates exchanged presents or cards with their children on the occasion of birthdays etc., and just under half of young offenders did so. These inmates were able to use their weekly earnings or private money to buy modest cards and presents in the prison canteen, or to make gifts in workshops, on education classes or in their cells.

Telephone calls

Card-operated pay telephones are installed in most prison establishments and prisoners may make calls from them during hours specified by the governor. Where the facility is heavily used, the governor may impose restrictions on the duration of calls allowed to each inmate. In practice, many inmates employ this means of communication to ensure they stay in regular (often daily) touch with their partners and children but the cost of phone cards on the whole limits the possibility of extensive use of this medium. At the time of writing a new 'pin phone' system, which replaces the card system, is being piloted with a view to implementation across the prison estate over the next two years. Each prisoner will have his own pin number and an established list of people he wishes to be able to telephone. This is intended to prevent the use of phone cards as currency within prisons, and the making of nuisance or other socially undesirable calls.

Phone calls provide a regular, easy, immediate and personal form of contact between inmate and child. However, some 15 per cent of adult inmates and almost half of young offenders giving information had no phone contact with their children. In contrast, 42 per cent of adults and 11 per cent of young offenders reported daily contact with their families by telephone. (One of those interviewed reported eight to ten brief calls daily.) As many as 83 per cent of adults and 48 per cent of young offenders who phoned their children said that they were in touch with them by this means at least once a week.

The value of this contact cannot be overestimated and a major issue for some inmates concerned the availability of phone cards to enable them to speak as frequently as they wanted. For those living at some distance from their families the expense was also an issue, as was the tension that can arise when inmates are feeling frustrated at waiting for another person to finish his call, a problem which was also strongly highlighted by inmates in the group interview. One person told us:

> There was a fellow inmate phoning home last night who got into a quarrel with his wife. He was also wanting to talk with his children. Another inmate passed by making a lot of noise and was asked to be quiet. This led to a row and then a fight between the two inmates, with much bruising and bloodshed.

However, three-quarters of partners made positive comments about the value of phone calls between father and child, compared with only 8 per cent who felt they were of 'no benefit'. The very positive response to phone calls endorses the inmates' views of their importance in maintaining contact with their child/children. Here are two examples:

> Phone calls are an important form of contact. Recently, association has been moved from twice to once a week which means prisoners can only phone once a week and then there is a big queue so the calls have to be short. Because this contact has felt crucial to us as a family, my husband has had to stop taking business education classes, which were going to be very useful to us – we formerly ran a small business but are now bankrupt and have to start up again – so that he can instead work as a cleaner on the wing which means he can, in fact, phone every day. These calls are very important to [my son] and encourage him to go on doing well at school even though his father is away. So this is an area that needs improvement in the system.

> Letters: lifeline to each other.

> Phone calls: nightly. There's a rota each night for the children. They upset Dad but help the family get through the day.

Tape recordings

Some children may be helped to remember their fathers by playing video-tapes, and occasionally audiotapes, which feature their father prior to imprisonment. In some prisons, fathers may also have audiotapes featuring their children's voices. Some fathers, however, have found the means to obtain tapes and record messages, songs or stories for their children. This has either taken place through individual initiatives with prison support, or through schemes such as one entitled 'Story Book Dad': staff from a charitable trust, together with the education and probation departments, utilised funding made available by the prison area manager to purchase a quantity of tapes and to assist fathers either in reading, singing nursery rhymes, or telling their own stories to their children. The original purpose of this scheme was to relieve the distress of younger children who were clearly missing their fathers a great deal.

To complement their communication by telephone, some adult inmates had, and played, audiotapes of their family. This constituted a minority of about one in seven of adults, a figure which contrasted markedly with those who possessed photographs of their children, who comprised nearly 90 per cent of all adult inmates Among young offenders, none had audiotapes but almost 80 per cent had a photograph. No inmates had videotapes of any kind. As the co-ordinator's case scenarios from the 'Story Book Dad' scheme show, tapes can, however, be an important means of contact for the children:

> The inmate's partner was unable to visit prison as she usually did. [New baby, new home.] Preschool child became upset and threw a tantrum because she wanted to see Daddy. This father had already sent two storybook tapes. Her mother said she could listen to him instead; at this point the tantrum stopped and the child sat and listened to the tape.

> This inmate is from overseas. His wife sends photocopies of stories from the children's favourite books and on the last visit she left a book. He reads stories and translates others. He said, 'I found out by joining a group of enthusiastic fathers that it's a good feeling to keep the best contact with your children, and it's definitely not silly to tape stories for kids like this.'

> One inmate told me of his small daughter, 'When she first got the tape she was freaked out and started to cry because the sound of my voice without me upset her. Now she listens to them again and again. She said one of the stories on the last tape was boring. So in the group we discussed choosing stories that had action and humour and that I enjoyed telling. It amazed me at the last visit. I told her to go and get a book we could share and she could read all the words.'

> Several fathers have said that the feedback they have is that the children look forward to getting the tapes addressed to themselves in envelopes that are often highly decorated, either with Dad's own drawings or

with stickers which we provide. They play the tapes over and over again, just as children will ask for the same story repeatedly.

In summary

Ordinary visits exist to implement the requirements of Prison Service Order no. 5. The family and children's visits and family learning programme examined for this study differ in title and emphasis, but all operate in the interests of strengthening family ties and, notably, those between father and child. These schemes are not dissimilar in terms of eligibility and process, though content and length of visit are more variable. The schemes enjoy the involvement of a wide range of personnel, including probation and prison officers, prison education staff, charitable organisation staff and volunteers. They have a 'start and stop' history because of ongoing security problems, which seem likely to continue, but are nevertheless popular with the committed staff who run them. Apart from the major concern of security, notably in relation to drug smuggling, other accompanying problems include effective scheme publicity, travel cost and time for partners, the shortage of committed uniformed staff, and children who become upset at parting from their fathers after experiencing renewal (or, for some, nascent) intensity of contact.

An additional area of concern which parenthood course staff mentioned, although visits scheme staff did not, might well be the inability of some of these close family contacts to continue when men moved to other prisons which did not run these enhanced visiting facilities. If the 'start and stop' trend is to be stemmed, schemes to be spread to other prisons and children to enjoy improved quality of access to their fathers as a result, then clearly there is a dual need for security obstacles to be overcome and scheme evaluation processes to be built in, and to be convincing in terms of their contribution to successful rehabilitation.

Non-face-to-face means of contact were seen by most involved parties as beneficial to the child, usually in a way which supplements and bridges visits. Telephone calls and letters, probably in that order, were viewed as especially facilitative to ongoing father–child relationships; their value cannot be overestimated. All these types of contact could benefit from specific review to consider ways of maximising their strengths and reducing negative and damaging factors.

CHAPTER FIVE

Families' Experiences of Father–Child Contact

The previous chapter made it apparent that non-face-to-face contact between children and imprisoned fathers is seen as extremely important by all parties concerned. Although this is occasionally the only form of contact enjoyed or chosen by inmates, it more frequently constitutes a vital supplement to the face-to-face contact provided by the prison visits system. As we have shown, however, the process of making a visit is not straightforward. It requires considerable planning, including the necessity to remove children from school if it is a weekday and a term-time period. It may also necessitate an injection of already overstretched family finances, if assistance with visits is not otherwise available, and frequently it will entail a long and tiring journey which may be stressful for both child/children and partner/carer. In discussing the experience of visiting in prison, other authors have noted:

> Prisons are carefully designed to prevent violence and escape. They are not designed to support self-esteem or to permit dignified human inter-action...Although prisons permit children to enter, they make no accom-modation for them. Children are expected to sit quietly, without toys or materials to occupy them, for anywhere from one to several hours. (Gamer and Schrader 1981, pp.203–204)

Things have improved over recent years in respect of child awareness, pro-vision of toys and so on, but it is nevertheless instructive to listen to the views and experiences of inmates, partners/carers and children, with respect to the range of visits available. Their feedback provides the key to assessing both the usefulness of the varied visiting provisions and the impact of these provisions on the maintenance and enhancement of relationships between imprisoned fathers and their children.

Likes about visits

By far the most frequent form of face-to-face contact used between children and their fathers is that of ordinary visits. All inmates visited by their children (90% of adults, 50% of young offenders) availed themselves of this facility. When asked what they liked about ordinary visits, a fifth of adult fathers specifically mentioned child-related aspects of their visit. These included the fact that they could: play with/relate to their children; be more natural with the family; exercise the father's role; or that their children could use the crèche/play facilities. Children's reactions, as reported by their fathers, were along similar lines and, as illustrated in Chapter 3, some of the younger children interviewed emphasised the importance of having toys, games and activity on visits. However, a fifth of adults and a third of young offenders could suggest nothing they liked, and this tended to relate to restrictions and lack of child-centred facilities in the ordinary visits settings.

In respect of children's and family visits, however, child-related reasons were far more commonly mentioned – again with references to being able to play with or relate to children, be more natural with the family, the provision of crèche/play facilities being noticeably frequent. (There are no comparable figures for young offenders, as no young offender institution offered either children's or family visits at that time.) In respect of these visits, however, additional advantages were cited. The following interview extracts show the benefits of reduced surveillance, the potential for working at relationships within the wider family and for activities to be shared as a family:

> I like them because they're not full of prison officers and I can pay full attention to the children. I feel closer to the kids and can actually play with them. In ordinary visits I'm so hampered that I don't feel like a dad and cannot act like a dad.

> Family visits have enabled me to heal my relationship with my parents. Ordinary visits reveal a very sincere expression of someone's feelings for you, that they are willing to go through that.

> I've used monthly children's visits elsewhere where there were gymnasium facilities. We loved them. I could play with the children and get to know them. There was much more contact. I became a person.

These three quotes demonstrate, in different ways, the humanising effect on both prisoner fathers and their families of more relaxed visiting facilities. For similar reasons, town visits and, for the minority who had experienced it, home leave were welcomed; inmates again referred to being 'more natural with the family'. In general, their responses focused rather more on 'family' than specifically 'children', probably because of the broader nature of the day release or home visit experience.

Dislikes about visits

Inmates were asked about their dislikes concerning each type of visit. There were small numbers who expressed no dislikes at all. However, many commented about lack of privacy, too much supervision, over-zealous security, the fact that their children were searched and sometimes distressed by this experience. The fathers in the group interview were particularly vehement about the importance of crèche facilities and about the inhibition to 'normal' ways of relating to their children of fixed seating arrangements.

Again, there is evidence here of fathers' concern about a lack of provision for their children, or other aspects of visits which interfere with what could otherwise be an opportunity for relaxed contact. Inmates commented particularly unfavourably on the restrictions on physical contact which some prisons imposed during visits. Some examples of these and other related concerns follow:

> I don't like the way visits are organised. There's nothing at all for children to play with. Kids get bored and start running about, screaming, falling over, making themselves a nuisance to other people. I feel frustrated as I can't get out of my seat to do things with the children or get up to control them. The children don't understand why

I can't get up and play with them. They are too young to understand. They just think Dad doesn't want to play with them.

It won't be a good environment to first see my child. The arrangements are too restricted; I won't be able to do the things I want to with the child – change its nappy, etc. I'm concerned about the lack of privacy at such an emotional time, and wonder how I will cope being presented with my new baby in a public place. (Inmate expected first child a week after the interview)

The effect of less physical contact is that children don't really understand that their father is not pushing them away – he just isn't allowed to cuddle as much as he wants to. Sometimes there's a tense atmosphere because of this non-cuddling relationship.

I dislike the length of time it sometimes takes to call me from the wing to visits. I've often had long waits, sometimes of two hours. They're much too petty here about the rules and regulations, e.g. not allowing you to raise your backside off the seat, not even to bend over to pick up your kiddie. The search procedure is degrading; my girlfriend dislikes the rub-down procedure. There's nothing for the kids to do and then they wonder why they run riot around the visiting room. They have a TV and video but it's never on. There's no privacy – the prison officers sit very close.

I can't take the children to the coffee bar. I have to stay seated, which is very restricting. No toys or anything for them to do. They treat visitors like criminals. My girlfriend hates that.

There are far too many restrictions. They are too heavy- handed in here, e.g. they tell you to stop kissing – threaten to end your visit if you even give your girlfriend a little kiss. They are paranoid about drugs in here. I have told my girlfriend not to bring the kids again now because it's too stressful, e.g. the last time she visited she waited from 1 pm to 3 pm to see me; then we only got an hour. The kids can't sit still for two hours. If she comes on her own she has to get back to collect the eldest from school and she is worried about getting back in time. If she has to wait hours it gets the visit off to a bad start; we both feel tense.

You can't move from your seat and can't even go to the coffee bar with your daughter. I don't have physical contact with my child for fear of the visit being terminated [if they suspect passing drugs]. There is absolutely nothing for kids to do. My daughter gets very bored. Other people's children 'run riot'. No toys. My daughter hangs on my arm all the visit saying she is bored.

I don't get the chance to see much of my child because after an initial hug she runs off because she is bored with sitting. The chairs are placed too far apart so I feel as if I'm shouting across the room. There is no privacy at all.

There are no toys in the visits room. Children get bored quickly. They're usually tired by the time they arrive because of the distance they have to travel and because they usually have had to wait quite a long time to be admitted. There are no facilities for children in the visits room and no proper food is served. The only food available is from vending machines. The visits hall is too small and gets very cramped. It's too much to expect small children to sit quietly throughout a two-hour visit; it's difficult for parents to keep children under control for the duration of the visit as they are bored. (Inmate's children are aged 4 and 3 years)

Clearly there is a major issue for the prison system, surrounding the primacy of security and the need to prevent drugs entering the establishment. However, its direct effect on the respondents quoted above, and on their interaction with their children, has been considerable. In contrast, those who had experienced children's, family and town visits or home leave had no such complaints, other than that they would have liked longer time with their families. Given the extremity of the two sets of experiences, it seems worth asking whether a better balance could be struck between security and child-oriented considerations for those who currently only have access to ordinary visits. If there were any doubts about the desirability of this, the following two sections show the importance of the quality of the visiting experience in helping or hindering continuing relationships between imprisoned father and child.

Helpfulness of visits in strengthening fathering role

Around a third of respondents considered that all visits had strengthened ties and relationships; a further 10 per cent considered that visits helped children remember their father, and a very small number referred to the disciplining of children as a way in which visits helped to support their partners. For one inmate, however, the prison's good intentions failed to work out as intended:

> For example, they did organise an all-day visit because of the distance the family has to travel. [Family very rarely visits because of the great distance and inconvenience of travelling.] But because they were short-staffed the morning visit was a closed visit with me behind glass. The children couldn't cope with it; they just sat and cried the whole time. They hadn't seen me for seven months and to see me behind glass was too distressing for them.

Another inmate, whose new baby had been brought to the prison to see him, nevertheless described the distress and anxiety he had felt when he learned that his wife had been having a problematic labour. He had, however, been helped and advised by one of the prison officers and reported that this had made him feel better:

> It's been awful – really awful – around the time of the birth when they told me something was wrong and she had been rushed in. It was a breech birth and she had to have a caesarean section. I was in a right state – not knowing what was happening – he being premature and all. Thankfully one of the prison officers had had the same experience; his wife had had a caesarean. He told me it would be OK and there was nothing to worry about. That made me feel a bit better. (At the time of interview, this inmate's child was six weeks old)

Other views of the helpfulness of ordinary visits were a mixture of positive and negative:

> It gives a chance for a cuddle and reassures the children that I'm OK. But I feel the phone is more use, more immediate. If they are playing up, put them on the phone, I can speak to them now.

> My girlfriend was dragged off a visit because I was feeling her tummy to feel the baby moving; they thought we were passing drugs. My girlfriend was taken out and stripped. She was almost nine months pregnant – the baby was born the next day. They let us resume the visit but she just cried all through the remainder of the visit. We complained but we never got a reply. The system is geared to your family breaking down. You have to have a pretty strong relationship to survive this. My girlfriend didn't want to visit again after that. It took her a long time to get over it. She only came because she knows how important it is for

me to see [daughter]. The whole thing was very humiliating and embarrassing for both of us.

Visits help in that I can still have some contact with them but they don't help in that I can't really have any influence on them as I am only with them two hours a week and can't even get out of my seat to play with them. Some officers understand and are sympathetic but in the main they don't seem to care. They don't think it's important so don't go out of their way to make the time more pleasant for children. If they were concerned about the effect of having a father in prison on children, then they would allow us to have more time with them.

Visits allow you to reassure children that you still exist and haven't done a bunk. They can allow you and your partner to express feelings for each other and this is reassuring to children that the family unit is intact.

In respect of those experiencing children's, family and town visits or home leave, a relatively high proportion commented on the way the visits strengthened ties or relationships, helped the child/children remember their fathers or the helpfulness of physical contact. Only one inmate mentioned disciplining children on these occasions.

Hindrance of visits to fathering role

Having invited respondents' views about the helpfulness of the range of visits to the father–child relationship, it was considered important to seek views about the potential hindrance to the relationship, particularly in view of the quite serious levels of distress reported by some participants. A minority of adults and young offenders alike described visits as causing 'no hindrance'. However, in respect of the majority that considered the visits to be a hindrance, some said this was because they were 'unable to relax and be natural', and others because of the lack of physical contact with their children:

It's supposed to hinder you, isn't it? It's part of the punishment – to disrupt family life. This sort of visiting system just causes divorces and separations – how can you have a proper relationship with your wife and kids when you see them for only two hours every two weeks? Wives get fed up with all the travelling, just to sit round a table for two hours. As for ordinary visits, you can't behave in ways that a normal, good dad would, so my son [aged 3] sees his dad acting as less than a father, and by the time he is four he might start to realise this, and this could break or damage our relationship.

At one visit all the [three] young children went scooting off in different directions. My wife can only pick up two at a time. I went up to the other and was told that I would be put on closed visits. They thought that I was passing drugs because I kept picking them up. I'm not into drugs; all I am interested in is my wife and kids. I want to be able to play with my kids and run about with them. When they get on to my wife or mess about with them by making them wait, it really winds me up and I get stressed out. At another visit one of the little children was crying, and I stood up to rock him, and was told to sit down. It's natural to rock and walk your baby if he's crying.

At one visit a prison officer started to shout at the children for running around. My girlfriend got angry and shouted back, 'Haven't you got any kids of your own? Can't you see they are bored? They have got nothing to do.' They said it wasn't their job to entertain kids, that was our job, but how can you when you can't stand up and they aren't allowed to bring any toys in and they don't provide any? Afterwards the POs took it out on me. They try to wind you up, or to make their point, they keep them waiting even longer next time. You can't win. I get so frustrated. Then my girlfriend said if it was going to be so stressful she wouldn't bring the kids again; then I get even more frustrated.

They need to be much more relaxed on visits. It's ridiculous them stopping you picking your kids up. What are you supposed to do? Just sit and look at them? A one-year-old wants to be everywhere and my arse has got to be on that seat. What's the point of them visiting if I can't hold them or play with them? I suppose it helps to some extent because if there were no visits I wouldn't see my kids at all. It's also too crowded in the visits room. You have one eye on them all the time, so you can't hold a decent conversation because you are seeing what they are up to. The worst thing is when they tell you to put your kids down.

Yes. You have no freedom to play with your kids. What can you do with a 14-month-old child who just wants to toddle around and you can't even get up from your seat?

It was clear from the above quotes that most of these respondents experienced the ordinary visits system, with its accompanying restrictions on contact and lack of play facilities, as quite punitive in nature and inhibiting to their fathering role. As far as children's and family visits were concerned, however, respondents tended to find no hindrance to their discharging of this role. A majority of the group interview respondents felt it was the nearest they were likely to get to normal family relationships within the prison setting. Town visits and home leave also prompted the relative satisfaction of inmates with these visiting arrangements. Adults and young offenders considered that in the main they offered 'no hindrance' to the fathering role.

Feelings about visits

Given the known emotional commitment to visits on the part of inmates, as well as the overall focus of this study, inmates were asked a series of questions about their own feelings and those of their partners and child/children before, during and after visits. In a general sense the opportunity to have visits is positively viewed:

> Good for all three. I have a '24/7 relationship'. I may be in prison but I am with my family 24 hours a day, 7 days a week.

> For days before a visit I think about seeing the children. They keep me going. I always look forward to seeing them.

> No matter how they are behaving, or what they have done [partner reports on their behaviour], it's always good to see them.

> When the visits are over I think about seeing them the next time. I can't wait to see them again. I'm upset because part of me is going away. The inmates who have kids understand, but no one else does.

Inmates' feelings before, during and after visits

For both adults and YOs who received visits, these were events to which they looked forward in great anticipation or about which they felt excited or 'high'. Thus for the vast majority visits were pleasurable in prospect. Only a small minority viewed them with apprehension, of which the following quote is an example:

I was excited about seeing them. I'd worried about them travelling all the way from [very distant home town] alone. I was anxious about how the visit would go.

During the visits themselves, the feelings of inmates from both age groups were also dominated by positive responses. Many reported being 'happy' or 'enjoying themselves', though only a small number described themselves as 'relaxed' within the given set of constraints. On the more negative side, some described themselves as 'tense'; two rather surprisingly said they were 'bored' and three 'frustrated'. Some men's excited anticipation was met with disappointment. The inmate whose family was travelling from a very distant home town said of the actuality:

Terrible – it was very distressing. The children cried all the time. It was terrible.

These general findings confirm very broadly all that inmates say about the break from an essentially unhappy experience that is afforded by visits from family and friends. For fathers, visits from their children can be particularly important and meaningful, even if separating at the end of the visit brings particular stress. When inmates from both groups were asked about their feelings after visits, only a handful felt 'energised' or 'buzzing' and a few said that the visit left them 'reflective'. Over half, however, said they were 'low' or 'depressed' and a fifth described themselves as 'upset'. The following quotes illustrate the feelings of these last two groups:

I get really down. I feel so bad I almost wish that the visit hadn't happened, but only almost.

I'm glad when they've gone. I feel very, very bad. I'm glad they've gone because it upsets the children too much. They were excited about coming but extremely distressed throughout and it took them a long time to settle down when they got back home.

I have to switch off. Don't get upset. I am a man aren't I?

The group interview with fathers tended to reflect the range of emotions about visits described above. For some, the 'seesaw' effect of meeting and then parting from their children was more than they could cope with. Others recognised and accepted that this was the price they had to pay for continuing to be fathers to their children. All of them felt that families should not have to be penalised for their offending.

Inmates' perceptions of partners'/carers' and children's feelings during visits

The attitudes and experiences of partners/child carers, and those of the children themselves, clearly make a crucial contribution to the quality of the visiting experience. Thus it was important to discover how inmates perceived their feelings about visits. We asked them how they thought partners/carers felt before, during and after visits of any kind. The vast majority of inmates thought that their partners/carers either looked forward to the visit or were 'excited' at the prospect. About 10 per cent thought partners were anxious about the visit and 5 per cent that they dreaded the journey.

Ex-partners were perceived to have additional, probably emotional, difficulties with the visiting process. For example:

> She doesn't like coming. In fact she often decides not to come on the day. It's stressful for her coming up – she doesn't relax during the visit and is always wanting to cut it short. After, she just wants to go home. The children love to come – they are always asking me when can they come up [when I'm on the phone to them]. (Ex-wife brings children 'once in a blue moon')

As Shaw has commented: 'The children of separated or divorced parents one of whom is in prison are in an ever less advantaged position than those of parents whose relationship survives an imprisonment' (Shaw 1992, p.107). It is hardly surprising that ex-partners have mixed feelings about bringing their children to visit their fathers in prison, particularly if their law-breaking has been a factor in the break-up of the relationship. It is indeed a positive stance for partners to take, to be willing to bring the children because they recognise the importance of the continuing father–child relationship. Shaw cites a range of court of appeal cases where separated/divorced prisoners who have applied for contact with their children have sometimes been successful and at others unsuccessful. Such prisoners may be seen to have forfeited their rights to contact with their children by reason of their criminal behaviour; in other cases this has not been seen as any bar to such contact. It does, however, have to be recognised that, even where an ex-partner does bring the children on visits, it is a doubly difficult experience for a child who has already had to adjust to separation from his/her father, then to have to accommodate the fact that this father is now also in prison. In such situations, one or both parents may be faced with the child's questioning about what has happened and why. As another author notes:

> We underestimate children's need for making sense of what has happened. This existential dimension where children dwell on issues concerning perspectives in life, other relationships, the future and themselves, easily goes unrecognised. If we do not recognise and communicate with children about these issues, they may feel alone or isolated. (Dyregrov 1994, p.180)

Considerable commitment is required from both parents, in these changed and uncertain circumstances, to focus on the child's needs for explanation and continued affirmation of love. Partners who undertake the difficult physical and emotional journey of prison visiting with their child/children are in particular need of 'quality time' to negotiate the complex range of interpersonal dynamics involved in this process.

In respect of the actual visits, most inmates tended to have a very positive view of their partners'/carers' feelings. Indeed, the majority of those in both adult and YO groups thought that their partner found the visits enjoyable or happy. A small number of adults described the partner/carer as 'anxious' or thought they disliked visiting. Among young offenders, only one described their partner as disliking the visit. The vast majority of inmates went on to report their partners feeling sad or depressed at leaving the visit to go home. A third believed that they had also to cope with their child/children's distress, or were tired because of the journey, or upset. Only 6 per cent of adults thought that their partner felt better for the visit. Among young offenders, none thought that their partner felt better for the visit and described them as upset, sad or depressed at leaving.

Clearly, a single visit precipitates a wide range of emotions in participants and, unsurprisingly, this is reflected in inmates' perceptions and observations of their children's reactions. Almost all inmates who responded described their children as 'excited' about or 'looking forward' to a visit. Only three adults and none of the young offenders referred to their children being 'anxious' before visits. In respect of their feelings during the visit, children were described by their inmate fathers as 'happy' or enjoying the visit in various ways. Only two adult inmates and one young offender described their child/children as 'anxious' or 'withdrawn' and a small number thought their children were 'bored'. Among the young offenders, the majority of those responding described what they perceived to be happy experiences for their child/children.

When inmates were asked how they thought their child/children felt after visits a different picture emerged. A quarter of adults responded, honestly, that they didn't know since they were not there to witness the longer term aftermath. However, of those venturing an opinion a high proportion described their child as 'sad', 'depressed at leaving', 'distressed' or 'clinging to me'. A fifth were described also as 'upset', compared with only about 10 per cent who were 'resigned' or 'accepting'. Only two fathers described their child/children as 'excited' after the visit. The inmates in the group interview felt that most of their children enjoyed visits, but a minority also described tears and clinging by their children when it was time to go. Many of them expressed frustration that they could not really know how the children coped once they had gone home, and recognised that this was a major responsibility for their partners.

Among the young offenders there was a similar pattern to the adults of describing children as sad, distressed, upset or tired; only one young offender reported his child to be 'excited' after visits.

Partners'/carers' and children's reactions to visits

When partners were asked about their preferred type of visit, the great majority of those who had used more than one type preferred children's or family visits. Unsurprisingly, the small proportion of the total who had used children's or family visits, but had also experienced town visits or home leave, expressed a preference for these latter facilities.

When asked their reasons for these preferences, partners tended to reflect the inmates' views that fathers could 'play with or relate to the child/children' or could 'be more natural with the family'. In one prison, the children's visits scheme takes the shape of children spending time exclusively with their father, while the partners/carers meet as a support group. At interview, members of this group expressed the view that it was very important for fathers to spend time alone with their children, since ordinary visits tended rather to be for the parents to spend time together. Also, on many prisons' ordinary visits dads had to stay seated at the table, whereas on the children's visits dads could move around and 'get on the floor for a rough and tumble'. Children were also reported by these partners/carers to prefer family or children's visits and for very similar reasons to those described above.

Where partners and children had used only one type of visit, usually ordinary visits, then their responses reflected this. They also valued the ability of inmates to play with or relate to the child/children and to be natural with the family, but a number of them, including the group respondents, specifically mentioned crèche or play facilities. Children's reported reactions were along similar lines. Two partners referred to their children's preference for the lighter uniforms worn by prison staff in the two private prisons since they looked less like police uniforms. This, however, was the only difference reported between private and state prison visiting schemes.

As far as partners' and children's dislikes were concerned, there was particular reference to the lack of crèche facilities, but also to privacy, a lack of food, limited toilet facilities, etc. Security measures of various kinds were also viewed negatively by around one-fifth of partners and were universally disliked by the group respondents, who also felt that precious visiting time was lost in the process of being searched, waiting to be searched and waiting around generally:

> I hate the waiting. Today we had to wait outside the main gate for 40 minutes on this very hot day, and had nowhere to sit or any toilet or refreshment facility. Some of the staff are rude. Also there are no facilities in the visits room, only vending machines and no proper food. The children are hungry because they haven't had lunch but there are only crisps and sweets available.

> There's nothing likeable. No privacy. Prison officers are always very close, and watching every move. There are no facilities at all for children. We had to wait after arriving. Myself and the baby were searched. Visits should start at 2 and sometimes we're kept waiting until nearly 3.

> There are no toilets in the visits hall. Sometimes I have to leave the baby in the visits hall if my little girl needs to be taken back to the waiting

area to use the toilet. I don't like having to be searched every time we go back to use the toilet. It's very slow getting in to visit. Sometimes it takes over an hour and we often miss part of the visit because they are very slow getting everyone through security.

When the 3-year-old saw people being 'rubbed down' and the PO didn't do it to her, she went up to him with her arms outstretched and said, 'Me too'.

Again, these quotes reflect distressing experiences for partners and their children, and a sense that they too are being punished for the prisoner's wrongdoing. It is unfortunate that such experiences may serve to reinforce society's existing negative images of prisoner fathers, both for children, partners and the fathers themselves. A child might reason that if the fathers merit disrespectful or insensitive treatment, then so perhaps do they as part of the same family. Children, and some partners too, are likely to look up to people in uniform. Thus, the behaviour of prison staff towards the person they know as father may have more effect on family dynamics than is immediately apparent. In a discussion of post-separation father–child involvement, (Ihinger-Tallman *et al.*) suggest that fathers' and their families' perceptions of their identity as fathers will inevitably be influenced by the opinions of others who are involved in arrangements surrounding contact. They describe this as a process of translation of fathers' identity into levels of involvement with their children:

Thus encouragement from important persons to continue paternal involvement will likely strengthen the translation process, whereas discouragement will weaken it. (Ihinger-Tallman *et al.* 1995, p.74)

This would suggest that prison staff who treat fathers and families with respect and show support for their continuing interaction are likely to aid the self-images of fathers, children and partners alike, thus increasing their motivation to develop and nurture their contact, despite the range of difficulties surrounding this process.

Partners were further asked about their own and their children's feelings before, during and after visits. Generally, partners were 'excited' or 'looking forward' to visits, though a number described themselves as 'anxious', 'unsure what to expect' or, indeed, dreading either the visit or the journey. Some group respondents reported anxiety about the searching process for them and the children – 'feeling like a criminal too'. Others said visiting had by now become routine and they had got over the anxiety stage. Only a minority of partners reported negative feelings during visits, but afterwards many said they felt 'sad', 'upset' or 'relieved', as shown in these examples:

> It's a mad rush but I look forward to coming and I come early, sometimes an hour before, in order not to miss a single second. During the visit the first half is news-giving and joking, but then it gets gloomy because we are coming to an end and we will have to wait a fortnight for the next visit. Afterwards I am worn out and tired because I had looked forward to it and it's all over so quickly. I feel depressed on the journey back.

> I like seeing him, but I worry about going to the prison. I was strip-searched. How could they do that to a woman who is heavily pregnant? I didn't want to go again after that, but worry about his state of mind if I don't.

> I enjoy seeing him but feel very tired afterwards. I feel drawn, empty, numb. I just have to get on with life. It's hard. At home we do everything together, the gardening, the shopping, etc. Now I feel so alone.

> I'm always upset afterwards and very tired – it's emotionally draining. I don't want to do anything when I get back. It lasts a day or so depending on how well the visit went.

Many of these comments are likely to be tied up with partners' feelings of responsibility and concern for the reactions of their children during visits. Nevertheless, with respect to their own perceptions of children's reported feelings, only a very small number were seen as anything other than positive at the prospect, this minority being reported to be 'anxious' or 'unenthusiastic'. During the visits, there were again very few children reported to be other than positive, though a few were said to be 'bored' or 'pleased at first then bored'. However, there were many more accounts of children feeling more negative after the visits. Many were said to be sad, upset, distressed, tearful or clinging; 10 per cent were described as tired. Some of the partners responded:

> They get very excited when their dad is due. The two boys are very pleased to see him and have lots to tell him but they still look to me for a framework. They start getting upset near the time they have to leave

and they get very upset at the station. They start rowing and bickering for the rest of the day. I have to referee. Next day they are more settled.

She loves seeing her dad. Even though she is only seven months I think she knows as soon as we get there that we are going to see [inmate]. Her face lights up when she sees him and she puts her arms out to him. She cries when we have to leave.

Before: they get excited – hyper – because they know they will see Dad. During: they are badly behaved, running about, fighting and shouting. After: they are tired and difficult. They ask awkward questions about why Dad can't come home.

Clearly, these partners/carers have to manage not only their own range of emotions about the visits, but also those of the children, whom they perceive typically to be excited at the prospect of and during the actual visiting event, but reacting in a variety of unhappy ways afterwards. This is reflected in their range of responses to our question as to whether the visiting arrangements were of help to the fathering role. Those who were positive nevertheless replied cautiously; some by making comparisons with visiting arrangements in other prisons where the inmate had been housed. Others referred to 'physical contact', mentioning that it 'strengthened ties or the relationship'; a few reported that it 'helps child/children remember their father'. Some partners told us:

Probably the best of the prisons I've been to. I like the way the play area is separate from the visits area – the children can come in when they want. It's the best prison for children's facilities. The other ones didn't cater for children at all. The children were 'bored out of their brains'. They just ate all the time – that's all there was for them to do.

Heaven, compared to [previous institution]. I used to cry every time I went there. I was strip-searched on several occasions and felt humiliated. The children (now aged 5 and 4) were also strip-searched. Nothing like that has happened here. I feel much happier bringing children to visit here. (Comments of child's grandmother who brings the children because the parents are long separated)

The way the visits are arranged are of no help. He can't see them much, even though we get three hours. I usually leave early because the kids are getting bored and the staff are getting on to them to sit down and be quiet. [Inmate] is always getting told off for getting off his seat to see to one of the babies. On one occasion our visit was terminated after only 15 minutes because he stood up to get one of them. Then he gets really stressed out and starts being rude to the officers which makes it worse.

When the child (now aged 2) was born [the inmate] was not informed of the delivery for some time afterwards even though the family had phoned the prison with the news. It was very hard for him, missing the child's birth, and he feels regret about that. When I visited for the first time after the birth, he wasn't allowed any physical contact with her because of the snake system. He felt awful, not being able to support me emotionally after the birth of the baby. There were no facilities for babies at that prison.

No, not particularly. They only see him for two hours. There should be arrangements for fathers and children to play together.

One partner summed up the whole dilemma of prison visiting with children very succinctly:

An enormous gap opens up between Dad and his children because of prison. It's a difficult choice, diabolical: to put children through the ordeal of visits into prison, or have them believe their dad isn't interested in them? To visit or not to visit? A decision I made [to visit]. But I felt I was left with all the responsibility.

In summary

Much of the foregoing information suggests that ordinary visits at least are a source of combined stress and happiness for the participants. They attract strong emotions because of what they can and cannot achieve. Joyful reunion takes place, but is brief, restricted, sometimes curtailed and can end, literally, in tears. Surveillance is high, demonstrations of physical affection are frequently prohibited for security reasons and children's play facilities are minimal or absent in many prisons. It is clear that these visits are crucial to the continuation of family relationships, but are arguably sometimes emotionally damaging for children. Nevertheless, a majority of adult prisoners, at least, was able to find something positive about ordinary visits. It is perhaps important also to comment that no appreciable difference between ordinary visits at state prisons and those at private prisons was identified. Those prisoners, partners and children who used children's and family visits, town visits and home leave appeared to find their relationships helped and supported by these occasional opportunities to relate to each other as a family in some semblance of normality.

These findings would suggest that there are very many partners/carers and children who are committed to the process of continuing the father–child relationship throughout the prison sentence – and that they are willing to endure a series of hurdles and stresses in order to further this endeavour as best they can. It is, however, apparent that ordinary visits cannot be guaranteed to be a positive experience, whereas the four other types of visit were almost universally described by all parties in appreciative terms. There is, thus, a need to generate a focus upon developing all visits into child-centred events in a way which does not compromise security considerations. As the succeeding chapter will show, initiatives both in the UK and the USA are being developed which have the potential both to support the family unit and to strengthen inmates' roles as fathers.

CHAPTER SIX

Formal and Informal Support Systems

This chapter draws on the views of prisoners, partners and staff about the provision and quality of formal support systems such as parenthood or fatherhood courses, voluntary bodies and statutory organisations such as the probation and social services. It considers the implications of these findings for interaction between such formal systems and the more informal support systems located in the wider community, notably within the family itself.

Parenthood courses

Interviews with ten involved staff and accompanying documentation from five adult and three YOI parenthood/fatherhood programmes provided the authors with information about this support facility. These programmes have been operating, in various forms, in some male adult and some young offender institutions for more than 15 years. In an earlier survey of parenthood training in YOIs, Caddle (1991) found 18 out of 29 YOIs providing such a facility. This followed an internal CEOB (Chief Education Officer's Branch of the Prison Service) survey which, at the end of 1988, had identified 20 such courses in YOIs. Some of these had been running for several years. The present survey identified 15 parenthood courses in YOIs at the end of 1996, which had grown to 18 two years later. Across the adult male prison system, this figure rose from 11 to 27 during the same period. Subsequently, Dennison and Lyon (2001), in their survey of 43 YOIs/prisons holding young male offenders, found only four reporting that they did not, never had and were not planning to run such courses. It is clear that their provision is growing across the prison estate and in YOIs particularly.

Both CEOB and Caddle found the length, content, process and teaching style of parenthood courses variable. A decade later, both our study and that of Dennison and Lyon (2001) found that this remains the case, though these courses and staff's awareness of the need for them appear to be on the increase, along with the growth of the prison estate during this period. In particular, almost all the private adult male prisons now run such courses.

Reasons/thinking behind the programmes

Most of the longer standing programmes began as a result of education, probation, other prison staff or external voluntary bodies such as New Bridge and the Ormiston Children and Families Trust identifying a need, particularly among young fathers, for some practical help and relationship advice in respect of their parenting role. They were aware that the time these fathers could spend with their children on visits was limited and as a result, in the words of one adult programme, aimed to 'improve relationships between the prisoner and his family by promoting responsible fatherhood through increased awareness of the experience and responsibility of parenthood'. Frequently, it has been the commitment and enthusiasm of these pioneering personnel that have ensured the programmes' success and continuity, in one case over a period of 13 years.

However, it is clear that the programmes which have sprung up from September 1997 onwards have almost all done so in response to Prison Service Instruction 57/1997 on the prison service core curriculum and thus, arguably, seek to bring together personal needs and educational attainment. 'Parentcraft' and 'family relationships' are both units of the 'social and life skills' programme and require a minimum of 20 contact hours. This can lead to accreditation through the Open College Network. Prison education departments may choose whether or not to offer these units and may also determine the process and content of delivery. Often they draw on specialists in the fields of child care, home economics, midwifery and health visiting. All prisoners across the board are expected to be given the opportunity to participate in the units offered. The overall aims of the 'social and life skills' programme are: the development of alternative self and society views; increase in self-esteem, self-confidence, social, personal and vocational competences; and the attainment of nationally recognised qualifications.

Programme leaders

Of the eight programmes studied, five were run by education department staff, one by prison probation staff and two by the staff of external voluntary bodies. Two of the five education-run programmes were operating the new 'parentcraft' unit and one the 'family relationships' unit in adult prisons. All three YOI programmes, while moving towards the prison service core curriculum requirements, remained needs-led, focused upon their original rationale, and making fatherhood or expectant fatherhood the major eligibility criterion.

Programme length and continuation

As mentioned above, the longest running of the eight programmes studied was 13 years and the shortest 12 months (the two operating the 'parentcraft' unit). A 'parenting skills' course in an adult prison, very popular with inmates, has been running for 5 years, and all the other programmes have been in existence for between 18 months and 2 years. Some programmes in other institutions which have been run successfully prior to this have ceased because of lack of numbers, lack of prioritised funds, or lack of staff to run them. All staff currently running programmes hope that they will continue indefinitely, but are fearful of the prisons ceasing to prioritise them, education contracts not being renewed and the potential for their own redeployment – though the latter is perhaps less the case for external voluntary bodies. However, the advantage of the new core curriculum requirements is that any education deliverer is likely to be contracted to run them and so where 'parentcraft' units have existed there is a reasonable chance that they will continue.

Programme funding

Where programmes are run by prison education departments, funding originates from the Home Office. All prison education is now contracted out to local further education (FE) colleges which provide staff to deliver a range of courses. Such colleges will have won tenders for Home Office funding to do this. Where probation, the chaplaincy or other sections of a prison run parenthood programmes, the funding comes from the area prison manager's budget, although the individual prison's management will have prioritised the need for such a programme. Thus, 'further funding is very much dependent on the good will of the governors' was the view of one of the programme leaders. Where external voluntary bodies come in to run programmes, the teaching staff are paid from that organisation's funds.

Organisation of programmes

Most inmates enter the programmes voluntarily via the sentence planning process, having had their attention drawn to them by personal officers, induction programmes, posters or other publicity within the prison. At one adult prison, staff from a local health trust worked in a multi-agency partnership to gain funding from the Queen's Nursing Institute that enabled them to run a 'parenting roadshow' with stalls, videos, playpacks, etc., which prisoner fathers and their families could attend (Evans 1998). This event was also used to encourage prisoners to sign up for the parenting programme, one of the leaflets reminding them that 'We are concerned with the health of children and families. We are not employed by the prison and everything you say to us is confidential'. At the other extreme of the voluntary/mandatory continuum, however, in one adult prison, men are obliged to attend the parenting programme if they have been referred for education and no other course is available to them. All staff interviewed saw motivation as a key factor in the ultimate success of these programmes, so the route via which men arrived was clearly important. One adult prison programme also viewed it as crucial to interview the applicants individually, in order to assess their suitability for the programme, which demanded of inmates a willingness to be open, frank and interactive in their discussion of fatherhood.

Programme content and delivery

Most programmes run for two to three hours per session and one, at a YOI, runs for a full day each week with parenting skills in the morning and practical parenting in the afternoon. Usually a single (often female) member of staff leads each session, but may sometimes bring in specialists; for example, a family court welfare officer runs one session of a six-session YOI programme. A typical programme may include discussion of planning for parenthood; coping with babies and under-fives; child discipline; the father's role; schooling; parenting teenagers; and stepparenting.

The input on 'parenting' or 'fathering' appears to range from a single session within a general course on family relationships to 50 contact hours over 10 weeks. It may occur weekly or bi-weekly over 10 to 12 weeks or it may, for example, take place on a full-time basis over a period of two weeks. In some cases there are entry criteria – sentence length, existing or expectant fatherhood status – and in others none. They may be predominantly practical, for example, cookery, baby care, family budgeting; predominantly focused on the father–child relationship in the context of child development; or a combination of the two.

Delivery style ranges from didactic to the more frequent participatory forum. Some teachers use toys, video, role play, groupwork techniques and, in a few cases, bring in their own children for the men to relate to and play with. Inmates' contributions to the course might include written work for assessment, with a certificate and/or accreditation, or simply verbal participation without the pressure of assessment attached. Some courses can only be joined at certain times of the year; others are organised on a 'roll on/roll off' basis so that joining and leaving times are flexible. Like Caddle (1991) and Dennison and Lyon (2001), we encountered general enthusiasm from both inmates and staff – who tend to be their 'product champions' – for the presence of these courses in the prison system. The quotations below illustrate the advantages of the programmes in the words of the staff leading them.

ADVANTAGES

1. Inmate backgrounds

One notable thing is the frequency with which inmates disclose being abused as children. It offers a release of emotion and frustration as well as support, shared information and feedback from the group. (Probation officer, adult prison)

2. Uniqueness

There is nothing else which examines family relationships and parental responsibilities. (Education co-ordinator 1, adult prison)

3. Intimate issues

It provides an opportunity to speak to a woman about very intimate issues in a way which they have often never learned to do, but needed to do, with their partners. (Education co-ordinator 2, adult prison)

4. Strategies and understanding

It gives them strategies to cope with behavioural problems and a better understanding of the needs of their children and partner. (Deputy education co-ordinator, YOI)

5. Play skills

I have just been showing them how to play with simple toys, how to engage babies and toddlers with these. Some of them just regress to babyhood themselves. You can see nobody ever played with them. Most of them are surprised that their babies can actually learn and receive pleasure from this kind of simple play. (Peripatetic teacher, charitable trust, YOI)

6. Peer group support

They are all Dads – it's a common bond. They're eager to be there and learn from us and each other. The baseline is they want to do it well – everyone wants to be a good parent. You can build on that. (Education co-ordinator 3, YOI)

7. Achievement

It's a forum for gaining factual information, practical skills, knowledge of legislation. They all get a certificate and some will get accreditation. (Education co-ordinator 4, adult prison)

PROBLEMS

The problems associated with some of the programmes are also summarised by their leaders.

1. Attendance problems

We have no control over their being 'shipped out' or kept away because they're wing cleaners, etc. (Programme tutor, adult prison)

2. Sex offenders

The attendance of sex offenders can be a problem, first with the reaction of other inmates and second with the tension between their offences and the course content (e.g. the opportunity/potential stimulus of looking at 'Mothercare' catalogues). (Education co-ordinator 4, adult prison)

3. Unreal setting

It sometimes feels unrealistic to try and develop their parenting abilities in a prison, particularly as some have not been good parents, and there is a tendency not to challenge this because of shortage of time and the need to maintain a positive atmosphere. (Probation officer 2, adult prison)

4. Intensity

It's the same person [me] doing it all the time. This is intensive and very personal. It's always my view they get. (Education co-ordinator 2, adult prison)

5. Security limitations

We used to include a visit to an outside playgroup but media attention and prison fears about security have meant this has had to stop. (Deputy education co-ordinator, YOI)

6. Lack of continuity

Where inmates leave the programme and move to other prisons they should be able to slot into new programmes but these are not always available. Inmates also need a 'follow-on' course or other support system to help keep their enthusiasm and momentum going up to release. At the moment it's 15 good weeks and then nothing. (Education co-ordinator 3, YOI)

GENERAL COMMENTS

A very, very good step forward for prison education. A great pity all prisons aren't running it.

Mandatory drug testing has changed the attitude towards parenting in prisons. The main emphasis now is to stop the flow of drugs into prison, so inevitably this affects visiting and how much contact the inmate can have with his children. We try to suggest new ways for fathers to interact with their children, but it's virtually impossible for them to put these ideas into practice. There's no privacy on visits and any physical contact is viewed with suspicion.

I would like a contact/networking system with others who run these programmes. We're all doing it in isolation and there is so much we could learn from each other about the best and most effective ways of delivering the programmes.

Thus, as with children's and family visits facilities, staff were very positive about the need for and effectiveness of these courses. However, they also expressed areas of concern which included inmate attendance constraints resulting from the exigencies of the prison system; the involvement of paedophile offenders in classes which concentrate on images of children; security limitations; opposition from some uniformed staff; and lack of continuity if attenders move on to other prisons. Staff tend to operate in isolation from those running parenthood programmes in other establishments and some networking with a mutual problem-solving approach could be helpful here. As with the children's/family visits schemes only one (Caddle 1991) has been externally evaluated, though much emphasis is placed upon inmate evaluations (almost always positive) at the end of programmes, and one internal multi-agency evaluation is also published (Evans 1998).

Inmates' views of the parenting programmes

In respect of the present study, 29 per cent of adult inmates and 81 per cent of YOI inmates had attended a parenting programme. Only a small percentage who could have attended chose not to do so, largely because they felt there was nothing the programme could teach them. The numbers participating (42 out of 144 adults and 30 out of 37 YOs) reflect the deliberate inclusion of eight such programmes in the study's establishment sample. However, in the case of the YOIs, only 57 per cent were located in establishments where programmes were currently being delivered, and some inmates had obviously attended them in other establishments, a majority of which were running them during the research period. Eighty per cent of the YOs who had attended programmes said they had changed the way they perceived their fathering role and expected this to impact upon their children; 64 per cent of adults shared this view. Of this 64 per cent, half reported that the programme had made them a better father, and other respondents had learned about child development, how to play and talk with their children and communicate with teenagers. Of the 80 per cent YOs whose perceptions had been changed by the programmes, half reported that they had learned baby-care skills (the majority having children under two years of age), and about child development; 14 per cent said they had learned about the importance of fathers as role models. Adult inmates told us:

> I got a lot from it. It was good to talk about how I felt about my children. It made me more determined to take my responsibilities as a parent seriously.

> It made me realise just how hard it has been for my wife and the pressure she has been under. It also made me begin to appreciate the time spent with my daughter more and how to see things more from her point of view, to get down to her level. It helped me to see just how I put things on her – e.g. if I'd had a bad week, I would take it out on her by being irritable; now I am better at not letting those feelings interfere with the visit.

> It was just good being able to talk – get things off my chest. They highlighted all the issues. I can't say that I learned anything I didn't already know, but I felt they actually acknowledged that some of us do care about our kids, that we are not all bastards.

> I have now started to write individual letters to my children to let them know that I care about them in a special way. It has helped me to communicate a lot better with them.

> At first, I didn't know what to expect. It was directed more towards communication – lots of useful things that I shall definitely use. I was at the birth, but somehow I couldn't quite come to terms with the fact that

my daughter was actually here, even though it's something we both have wanted for a long time. Doing a course and sharing things with the others made it all seem more real. I am now aware of what I am missing and it makes me feel sick, but if I dwell on it I shall just get depressed so I try to look forward, plan to be a good dad in the future. It's made me see life differently. I have got to be there for her now. No excuses.

I went along to see if there was anything I could pick up. I was surprised how good it was. Really it was child psychology. The most important thing I learned was recognising problems and ways of discussing them.

It's helped me to understand my children a little bit better. I now try to look at the reasons behind their behaviour. I don't suppose it's changed my view dramatically but there are changes I am going to make. I am going to send the book to my wife. We both need to make changes to make it work. I would say the course has educated me to be a better father.

The following written set of evaluative comments from those who had completed one YOI programme is also broadly representative.

Everything on this course has given me a lot more of a view on being a parent. I really feel that after doing this course it has made me understand how important a father really is.

The course was excellent in all areas. It was very relaxing and easy to take in the information that was given.

All the health and safety tips were very good, especially the poisonous plants which shocked me.

I thought that the information about toys for children and games we can play was good.

One thing I won't forget is to get a smoke alarm.

How to look after the baby safely. How to give your baby a good life.

That I should discuss my problems with my girlfriend to maintain a strong relationship.

How to be a better father upon my release – i.e. give my child a better life.

The course makes me feel more like a father, to be told how to get more love from my child, to know about ups and downs due to birth.

I have enjoyed my parenthood classes since day one and have learned many different and useful things including buying a smoke alarm could save my family's life, what to do if my kid hurt herself or took some pills. Some subjects shocked me. The video on child sexual abuse made me feel very angry but frightened. (Several participants referred to this.) But I liked the atmosphere and I got a lot of confidence from the course.

Nothing poor about the course (again a general view).

Where inmates reported a change, they were asked what kind of changes had been brought about by the course. For the adult inmates, there were 31 reporting a change of some kind and of these half said that the course had 'made me a better father'. Others said they had learned about child development, how to play with children, talk to their children, or communicate with teenagers. One said the course had:

…made me aware – rather late – of my shortcomings and this is why I want in future to be in a better relationship with my children.

Another felt it had:

…made me more aware of problems facing my children and my partner, and the need to look at things from their aspects. [It] gave me a range of techniques for dealing with the children and how to cope with their questions, etc. A really good course. Taught me a few things.

Among the 30 YOs who had taken a course, high proportions reported having learned about child development (16), or learned skills in dealing with babies (15); seven said that the course had 'made me a better father' and five reported learning 'about fathers as role models'. It was important, also, to start making changes now.

I used to think I could teach them, for example, to swim tomorrow. You can always do it later – but later doesn't always come. Kids grow up so fast you need to do things with them now, not put things off.

Another young offender had been attending a course when he was transferred to a different establishment where no course was available. His reaction was, 'If they did another course here, I'd go on it.' This young man pointed out that a folder holding his work on an English course at his previous establishment had been forwarded to his new one, so his 'parentcraft' folder could also have been sent on. Another young offender said:

> It's not the parenting classes that have changed my attitude, it's being in prison. I have had a lot of time to think about my responsibility towards her [nine-month-old daughter being looked after by inmate's mother]. It's time to stop acting like a kid and get on with my life. That includes her [daughter].

Possibly, the courses taken by young offenders reflected the infancy of many of the children concerned and the need among these young men for practical help in dealing with babies and information about child development.

Partners' views of the parenting programmes

Clearly these programmes are very popular with inmates and appear to make a significant impact, particularly on young offenders who tend to be new fathers. Unfortunately, none of the children interviewed for the present study had fathers who had been to parenting programmes, partly because children of the preponderance of YO programme attenders would have been too young to include in the sample of children to be interviewed. It would also have been quite hard for children to evaluate the effects of a programme upon their father's relationship with them. Partners/carers were, however, asked if there was anything apart from conventional contact systems which they thought had helped the inmate with his fathering role. While 77 per cent (with the addition of the 7 group respondents) knew of nothing, 12 per cent referred to parenting classes, and their illustrative quotations showed how fathers had communicated their new learning to their partners and, in two cases, had used it to advise them about child-rearing practices:

> He told me all about it and how it helped him to think differently about family problems. He would say, 'They are only doing that [playing up or whatever] because they need attention.' He says there's no point in yelling or smacking; move them out of the situation or occupy them with something else. That's been very helpful to me because he's seeing it from a different angle. He's very patient with the children.

He sent me the certificate [from parenting class] to show me. He learnt a few practical things but he's got no idea what to do with real babies. (Inmate has two young children who have only visited him once. Partner describes herself as 'ex-fiancée'.)

[Inmate] enjoyed it. Then he thought he knew more than me. He started telling me when to wind [baby aged 12 months], what he should weigh, etc.

He told me the parenthood course had been good and taught him a lot. He used to be a 'Jack the Lad' before he went down. He says he understands now, and things will be different when he comes out.

Overall then, inmate and partner evaluation was positive; staff too were positive and enthusiastic. This applied equally to state and privately run prisons between which there was no appreciable difference. Importantly, inmates both at programme end points within this study and six months after release in Dennison's and Lyon's study (2001) were able to remember key pieces of learning that they had taken from the fatherhood programmes. These findings would suggest that further support on release would continue to enhance their ability to sustain positive relationships with their children. Here, however, the picture is less straightforward.

Inmates' links with helping agencies/organisations

There are a number of welfare agencies or organisations established to help inmates and their families during and after sentence. Some of these are provided by the state, for example, local probation services, social services departments, or the assisted visits scheme operated by the Department of Social Security. Other help is provided by voluntary bodies such as Help and Advice Line for Offenders and Wives (HALOW), Alcoholics Anonymous (AA) and a range of other advice and counselling services.

When each inmate was asked of his links with such agencies or organisations, it was striking that 42 per cent of adult inmates and 30 per cent of young offenders said that they had no links with any such body. Other inmates specially mentioned the probation service and, given its statutory involvement with prisoners both during and after sentence, where no mention was made of the probation service then the inmate was prompted by the interviewer. A total of 38 per cent of adults and 59 per cent of young offenders mentioned their home probation service, though only 18 per cent and 16 per cent respectively considered that the service was helpful to their families in the home area. The probation service within prison was mentioned by only 16 per cent of adult inmates and a mere 8 per cent of young offenders. Among each type of offender, a substantial minority reported that they found the probation service unhelpful. Two contrasting views follow.

> Yes, I have counselling from the chaplaincy and talk to a prison visitor and the Samaritans. My field probation officer is good.

> I'm supposed to have a probation officer, but they don't seem to want to know. You are pretty much on your own.

Turning to other links, there were relatively few with voluntary organisations of any kind. When inmates were asked about their families' links with helping agencies or organisations, about 50 per cent of the adult inmates and young offenders reported no links of any kind. None of the group respondents reported any links with helping organisations, but it is possible that peer group pressure operated to prevent individuals admitting to what might be seen as a weakness.

Among other agencies, 8 per cent of the families of inmate offenders were reported to have received help from social services but no other state or voluntary agency received many mentions from anyone. Even then, there could be concerns on the part of inmates. For example, one said:

> No. We don't want social services or anyone else interfering and checking up on the children. She's managing fine and I'll be out to help her soon.

Of course, it is possible that the inmate knew of agencies which might be helpful but with which he was not in touch for some reason. When questioned about this, a very clear picture was revealed of most inmates (88% adults) and (84% young offenders) knowing of no other agencies. A handful knew about the home probation service, a counselling service or other voluntary agency. Similarly, when asked about other agencies known to the inmate which might be helpful to the family but with which the family was not in touch there was again a high proportion of 'none known' responses (86% of adults and 78% of young offenders). For example, we were told:

I don't get any help, but there should be some sort of support system for prisoners and their families.

No contact with anyone. There should be information to all prisoners and families about the help that is available.

The picture that emerges from the questions about links of inmates with helping agencies is that very little help was felt to be received. In a number of cases it was clear that the inmate preferred no link for himself or his family and possibly had rejected overtures of help. One said:

No, I don't need no help. I'm the one that has to change.

The impression given, however, was that a high proportion of inmates were unaware of what help might be available, were not specifically seeking help, and generally had a low expectation of what might be done to help them or their families during sentence or on release.

Families' links with helping agencies

Having asked inmates, their partners were also questioned about the families' links with agencies or organisations which might help. Interviewees' responses clearly confirm the situation reported by inmates. Thus, 64 per cent said that they had no links with any agency or organisation, a situation which some 17 per cent said they preferred. A further 17 per cent said that they had, or had had, links with the probation service. None of the group respondents had any links with any agency, including the probation service. Among the positive comments were the following:

Probation and social services are a big support to me but I don't think it's true for everyone. Families should be able to count on this.

Letters and good contact from the probation officer are also a big help to us. She visits [inmate] and us and rings me at least once a month.

[Inmate's] probation officer comes to see me every six months or so after having seen [the inmate]. Rings me, gives me updates. It's very good and I know I can always ask for help if I need it.

And on the more negative side:

[Inmate] wrote to his probation officer, who didn't offer help when he asked for it. He didn't reply to his letter.

I am sure there are some [helping agencies] and I meant to find out because I was very upset and feeling alone at the beginning and it would have really helped to have talked to others in the same boat. If the probation officers had given me a list of agencies to contact I would definitely have done so. Now it's too late; he's nearly at the end of his sentence.

The probation service hasn't been in touch. I phoned them, they arranged to do a home visit but didn't. I'm scared to go to social services in case they take the children away. I know that there's an information booklet available; it's given to prisoners but not wives. The Prison Reform Trust publish it and I wrote and got it; I needed the information in it with useful addresses for support.

A link with the probation service should be a requirement and information provision also.

It is of interest that a few prisoner/partner self-help groups do exist across the country, but none of our respondent partners mentioned them. However, after the partner/carer group interview, group members apparently reported to the co-ordinating probation officer that they had enjoyed this opportunity to share views and experiences and would like to do so again in the future for mutual support purposes.

The partners were also asked about links of the inmate with agencies or organisations that might help him and the family after release. Here again, there was a high proportion responding that there were no links (47%); 21 per cent had, or had had, links with the probation service in prison and 13 per cent with the home probation service. Apart from this, there were virtually no other reported links.

It is striking that the support which is often assumed to be provided by the probation service and by welfare organisations in the community is so frequently absent when inmates or families are reporting on their links with agencies. Where probation support was offered after release, partners' responses were varied:

He should see a probation officer once a week for three months after release. [Inmate] needs a good firm hand, especially with his driving. The supervision period should go on longer.

He has a probation officer but he doesn't talk about it to me. I believe that he gets plenty of support when it's me that is in need of support.

Given the statutory involvement of the probation service with YOs and adult prisoners serving over 12 months, the level of linkage perceived by respondents is surprisingly low. Other minority links, mentioned by both prisoners and partners in less than 8 per cent of cases, included social services departments, the assisted visits scheme (Department of Social Security), counselling services, and other voluntary bodies such as HALOW and AA. When asked if they knew of any other supportive agency with which they might be in touch, 88 per cent of adult inmates, 84 per cent of YOs and 82 per cent of partners said they knew of none. This is significant in the light of a range of prisoner and partner self-help groups which exist across the country (HM Prison Service 1995) and exhortation for the probation service to facilitate prisoners' families' access to them (Codd 1998).

The overall picture emerging from these findings is that adult inmates and partners/carers felt that very little help was received from potentially supportive agencies. This picture is not dissimilar from that revealed in the small-scale follow-up of prisoner fathers by Richards *et al.* (1994) who found only 25 per cent of men receiving help from the probation service and 13 per cent from social services after release. The one exception in the present study was the 59 per cent of YOs who had links with their home probation service (although 27 per cent described this as unhelpful).

The picture also reveals that a high proportion of inmates and partners are largely unaware of what help might be available, and generally have a low expectation of what anyone other than themselves might do to assist them or their families during sentence or after release. As recounted in Chapter 2, this low expectation was also reflected by prisoners when they were asked what could be done in prison and after release to help them to get nearer to their 'ideal' of a father. In respect of both questions, 58 per cent of adults and 43 per cent of YOs answered that nothing could be done, and they felt it was up to them to achieve this position. Interestingly, the next most frequent answers were parenting courses, from 16 per cent of YOs, and children's/family visits from 9 per cent of adults.

Integrating support systems

There are two clear sets of implications from the findings about other formal support systems in this section. The first is that parenting programmes are a burgeoning success story in the prison system, especially in YOIs, and that participants feel they learn a great deal about the practical and psychological tasks of parenting. The second is that, again with the exception of YOs' links with home probation services, the majority of inmates and partners/carers do not receive, turn to or know about organisations which might support them during and after the period of imprisonment.

A landscape of restricted statutory and unpublicised voluntary help emerges, with inmates and partners/carers having low expectations of such help. It is arguable that self-sufficiency is preferable, and certainly a minority of respondents took this position. It is arguable too that the reality of the present state of affairs is that most fathers in the present study were succeeding in maintaining contact (if of low quality) with their children via conventional prison-based support systems, and the goodwill of their families, who often availed themselves of these systems at considerable personal and financial cost. It is interesting too that the formal support and education for the parenting role provided by the parenting programmes is one which, if implemented in practice, could also lead to further family self-sufficiency. This suggests that there is scope for a firmer sense of partnership between formal and informal support systems, so that a clear path can be plotted from one to the other, with the dual aim of child–father relationship sustenance and prisoner rehabilitation within his own most likely source of practical and emotional support and encouragement – the family.

Within the partnership framework described above and with some modest resource injection, the kind of integrated support programme which operates in parts of the USA to meet the needs of prisoners, partners/carers, and particularly children at different developmental stages, could well be in embryo. Weissman and LaRue (1998), for example, describe a family support programme, one part of which helps adolescents to deal with isolation and shame, and to make positive choices about their own behaviour and responses, by equipping themselves with knowledge about imprisonment and the law. Potentially this enables them, at their young adult stage of development, to find ways of interacting more comfortably with younger children, with their peers and with adults in discussing their imprisoned parent. In this way, the formal support system consciously nurtures the informal support system.

Other US support groups catering for school-age children both at junior and middle school level have also reported improved class behaviour, attendance grades and friendships (Johnson, Selber and Lauderdale 1998). These authors argue persuasively for the integration of theoretical understandings about recidivism and the effects of disrupted child–parent relationships into a systematic social support framework which provides a dual focus on offender and family in the joint interests of child–family stability and reduced offending rates.

Taking up the support concept, Seymour (1998) calls for more effective agency collaboration and more detailed research, including reliable population statistics and longitudinal follow-up studies. She points out that few studies have employed standardised assessments of children or, indeed, sought to gain data direct from the children themselves:

> To fully understand the needs of children with incarcerated parents, the child welfare community will need to promote and undertake quantitative and qualitative research on the effect of parental incarceration on children. Ideally, this research will include sufficient sample size, employ adequate comparison groups, gather information directly from children, and follow subjects for a substantial length of time. (Seymour 1998, p.478)

Other national bodies which have brought together academics, professionals, the voluntary sector and lay people to support programmes of research and action in this field include those in Scotland, Northern Ireland, Australia, Holland and France. The Scottish Forum on Prisons and Families commissioned an important qualitative study of prisoner–family contact funded by Save the Children and the Scottish Prison Service Research Unit (Peart and Asquith 1992), while the work of the earlier Scottish Consultative Group on Prisons and Families on health, social and education needs of parents and children is described in Shaw's edited volume (Anderson *et al.* 1992).

In Northern Ireland, the Northern Ireland Association for the Care and Resettlement of Offenders (NIACRO) conducted a survey of prisoners' wives, who reported high percentages of anger and depression in their children, and published a survival guide for families (Horner 1994). Subsequently, NIACRO organised a residential weekend for a group of prisoners' children. During this weekend the children talked with relief about their emotional difficulties, which normally they felt constrained to keep secret. They also made a seven-and-a-half-minute video giving voice to their concerns, now used to help other families of prisoners (Cunningham and Bryson 1997).

In Australia the Children of Prisoners Support Group pushed for action to implement research findings on the need for improved facilities for prisoners' families (Hounslow *et al.* 1982). As Lloyd (1995) reports, the Dutch probation service has helped to establish a mentor service for children of imprisoned fathers (Holwerda 1994) and the voluntary organisation 'De Vereniging Relaties van Gedetineerden' has published research on prisoners' families (Haar ter and Moerings 1991). France has a very active support organisation, 'Relais Enfants–Parents', which has also been responsible for a series of European conferences leading to the setting up of a European network of prisoners' families' support organisations. A number of the conference papers, bringing together research and practice, have been published (e.g. Michaud 1992).

In the UK, the 1996 North Eastern Prison After Care Society (NEPACS) Conference, for example, included contributions from Lloyd (1997), Pellegrini (1997) and Shaw (1997), whose research and publications have been cited earlier. Other speakers at this conference added relatively new information to the children of prisoners debate. Philbrick, a child psychiatrist, for example, surmised that 30 per cent of prisoners' children will have significant health problems, as compared with 10 per cent of the general child population (Philbrick 1997). This supports earlier findings about childhood loss and disadvantage as indicators of poor mental health in the future (Brown, Harris and Bifulco 1986; Cadoret *et al.* 1985). Moore, a primary special needs teacher, presented and discussed the findings from his earlier research (Moore 1988, 1992) which concluded that 90 per cent of children with imprisoned parents were not known as such to their teachers, though primary school teachers and teachers in their thirties were more likely than their other colleagues to be aware of this feature of a child's life. Individual rights and confidentiality were emphasised as key factors in dealing appropriately with children and parents in this situation (Moore 1997). Moore's research was later drawn upon in the publication of Save the Children's resource pack for teachers, *Working with Children of Prisoners* (Ramsden 1998). This document, steered by a range of interested individuals and organisations, began by stating that its origins lay in research and information generated by relevant projects and conferences, of which the NEPACS 1996 conference was a notable example. A summing up of this conference's discussions and findings concluded:

> Conference members believed that quality matters at least as much as quantity of visits for the child and that an energetic vigilance is required to defend existing good quality projects, to press for a generally higher standard of provision for children visiting prisons, and to look for further ways of confirming and strengthening family relationships for the child. (NEPACS 1997, p.106)

The national organisation which embodies this ethos within the UK is the Federation of Prisoners' Families Support Groups (FPFSG), which has the following stated aims:

> 1. To encourage and promote the development of a nationwide network of support groups and services for prisoners' families.
>
> 2. To act as a voice for prisoners' families and represent their views and concerns to the Prison Service and other agencies.
>
> 3. To publicise issues affecting prisoners' families.
>
> 4. To promote the just treatment of prisoners' families by the prison system and by society. (FPFSG 1999, p.3)

FPFSG seeks to implement these aims by providing advice, encouragement and good practice guidelines to those wishing to develop services to prisoners' families, to the probation service, researchers, and so on. It organises conferences to address issues of current concern and produces a range of publications, including a newsletter, *Action for Prisoners' Families*, and a national directory for prisoners' families. It works with the media to increase the public's understanding of the needs of prisoners' families. It engages in policy consultation and training for members and provides resource materials for students and researchers. However, like the support groups which it exists to advise, the FPFSG is reliant on charity funding and, because of the relative unpopularity of its clientele, is not an obvious target for media or political plaudits. Thus, as the former Chief Inspector of Prisons, Sir David Ramsbotham, noted, the federation is 'unsung, because the cause is not one that attracts public or media attention'. Nevertheless, as he goes on to point out: 'By helping families to cope with their additional problems, the Federation is contributing to the fight on crime as much as any other organisation connected with the criminal justice system...' (FPFSG 1999, p.2).

In summary

As Ramsbotham's observations clearly imply – and indeed as research cited earlier in this volume has shown – the family is frequently the key factor in a prisoner's successful rehabilitation. The most obvious means to mobilise it as a resource is proactively to include it as a partner in a tripartite programme of support, whose other two constituents would be the formal frameworks provided by the statutory services (notably prison and probation), and the less formal but potentially more individually tailored services provided by the voluntary sector. Such a framework would afford family relationships, and all the individuals within them, not least the prisoner and child, the respect which encourages people to take advantage of increased knowledge and choice. In this way they would be empowered to form their own decisions about future action, in line with the expressed preferences of many participants in our research.

CHAPTER SEVEN

Strategies for Change

The foregoing chapters have drawn upon existing literature and practice, and upon the authors' own in-depth study of prisoners, families and staff, to present a picture of the range and quality of provision which is available to support the continuation of child/imprisoned father relationships. It has deliberately afforded considerable space to the little-heard views of inmate fathers, partners/carers and their children; it has represented the expressed views of staff closely involved with formal support systems. A range of models of contact, of good and bad father–child experiences, has been delineated. There are some clear success stories, such as fatherhood courses and children's and family visits. Obviously, these need to be developed and built upon for more imprisoned fathers and children. Equally, we have also heard some sad and distressed stories which, in some cases, were damaging to the child and undoubtedly call for an improved and more imaginative set of responses, if society's duty to observe children's rights and needs, as set out in Chapter 1, is properly to be discharged. In our study, we asked respondents themselves to suggest ways forward and, in assessing strategies for change, this chapter will draw on the ideas they proffered as well as considering other implications of the background evidence in this field.

Respondent suggestions for improvement

The section on respondents' views about contact provision, within Chapter 4, has already inferred something of their suggestions for improvement in relation to visits and other forms of contact. These, and staff views about parenting programmes and visits schemes, will be briefly reiterated in this final discussion section in considering other ideas elicited from respondents about potential improvements to facilitate the parenting role of imprisoned fathers.

Resources within and beyond the prison

It will be recalled that when inmates were asked what could be done to help them get closer to their expressed 'ideal' of a father, the highest category of answer both in relation to the current sentence and after release was 'nothing'. Beyond this, an increase in availability of children's visits and YOs' parenting programmes in particular had been suggested. The next most frequent answer was access to education and/or employment training. Other suggestions included longer visits, more home leave, counselling services and alcohol/drugs rehabilitation facilities.

As observed earlier in this volume, the 'nothing' answer appeared to arise from a desire to manage without help, a sense of resignation that no support was available even if the inmate wanted it or, in some cases, both. This told its own story about the negative perceptions of such help as was available: for example, the fear of social workers removing children rather than supporting families to stay together; and perhaps about the quantity and quality of information about support services which actually reaches prisoner fathers.

In respect of longer visits, home leave and the 'halfway house' of town visits, it is not, of course, surprising that prisoners want more opportunity to be with their families. Certainly the last two types of visit represent temporary liberty which is bound to be especially attractive. However, it may be unhelpful to continue categorising them as privileges to be earned when, clearly, any time spent maintaining and rebuilding family relationships is time which may well contribute to greater stability in the post-release resettlement process. The majority of prisoners are not a danger to society; the rate of absconding and offending on temporary release is extremely low. The prison service now compiles regular and rigorous risk assessments on prisoners. Those assessed as at low risk of reoffending in a serious way could reasonably be released for single days and weekends much earlier than is now the case. This is not a 'let-off' for anyone when the prisoner always has to return to prison. It does, however, nurture father–child and wider family relationships in their natural setting and strengthens the greatest protective factor in all their lives – for the child, continuity of paternal love, and for the prisoner, stability and responsibility which help guard against reoffending.

Only a small number of inmates had access to counselling or alcohol/drug rehabilitation facilities while they were in prison, though current plans to extend accredited group programmes which address addiction may ultimately be of help here. Few prisons, however, possess the counselling or other one-to-one services which were referred to. Chaplains may provide these in a religious/spiritual context. Probation officers within prisons may also offer one-to-one support in certain cases, but the prevalence of this has reduced across the board since the advent of the 'effective practice' initiative (Chapman and Hough 1998) which draws on research meta-analysis to endorse an increase in the use of cognitive behavioural groupwork programmes at the expense of more traditional psychodynamic methods. A service of this kind may be resource-intensive, but it is nevertheless much needed. Our experience as researchers is that many prisoners are crying out to be listened to in a peaceful, confidential, reflective context. Beyond prison, there may be more resources available in respect of problems relating to addiction and other counselling needs, but eligibility criteria make access to them problematic. Recently released prisoners frequently fall between the two stools of needing to have reoffended to attract assessment and intervention, or having sufficient income to pay to acquire help. At a time when, perhaps, they are most motivated to work on their problems in order to stay out of the prison experience from which they have been released, the nearest they may get to receiving direct help is being placed on a waiting list. This is a prime example of the family as an informal support system, very much needing an injection of help from a formal support system. When the latter is not available, it leaves an unfilled hole in the informal system, which in turn inevitably sags for lack of adequate support.

The access to education, training and employment opportunities, both within and beyond prison, which some inmates saw as helping them to become better fathers, will clearly constitute a huge benefit to families and fathers if its availability can be widened. Very many offenders are unemployed, unskilled, unqualified, have literacy and numeracy problems and related low self-esteem. As Marsiglio (1995) has noted, the processes by which men internalise particular fatherhood images and develop their perceptions of father status and its accompanying roles are crucial here. Despite modern principles surrounding gender equality in parenting, cultural and media images of fathers as providers are still very strong. The low self-esteem of many prisoners may well be related to their perceptions of their capacity as providers, which in turn may relate to their self-image as fathers. (Some of them, after all, have even failed in their intention to provide through committing crime.) These images are also likely to depend on their response to real or imagined expectations of others' responses to them, as prisoners who have failed in all their roles as parent, partner and provider. As one researcher writes of young fathers in particular:

> Fatherhood occurs to men who often have a personal biography that poorly equips them to act on their intentions, even when their intentions to do for their children are strongly felt, and fatherhood takes place in a culture where the gap between good intentions and good performance is widely recognized. (Furstenberg 1995, p.144)

Employment and qualifications do not necessarily guarantee prevention of reoffending, but they are a known protective factor. A prison sentence is a golden opportunity for someone who has never learned to spend time productively to be provided with a sustained period of tailored support which would follow them through to the post-release period, to try to ensure that they were gainfully occupied, thus becoming self-respecting, and providing for their family, as so many of them told us they wanted to do.

Strengthening family ties

Overall, these developments of inmates' ideas suggest very clearly that family ties should be strengthened in a range of direct and indirect ways, rather than becoming diminished during a prison sentence. Other suggestions made by some inmates and partners included weekend imprisonment, so that family responsibilities could be carried out during the week, an income could be earned to support the family and the complexity of families visiting prisons avoided. Even the desirability of this in terms of relieving the burden on the taxpayer was referred to. Some also considered that parenting programmes should be made much more widely available and inmates encouraged to attend them. One inmate felt that more change could take place within the visits system if it wasn't for politics:

> Prison staff should let you give kids presents on their birthdays. There should be all-day visits with the family. The government is splitting families up by vote-grabbing and making families suffer. Making the next generation criminals.

Comments from the children certainly reinforced the idea that they would like longer and more frequent contact with their fathers. While some could receive birthday presents, others could not understand why this was not possible.

When partners/carers were similarly asked for other comments and suggestions about imprisoned fathers and their children generally, a small number considered that their children were faring better for having their fathers away, and this should not be overlooked in that minority of situations where children are clearly being damaged in some way by continuing contact with their imprisoned fathers. An example where the partner clearly felt the child was better off not seeing her father too often is as follows:

> We've been separated since [child] was a baby so she's accustomed to not seeing her dad daily; hence there's no impact on schooling or health or behaviour. Actually, she's been better since [inmate] was in prison. We have avoided contradictory instructions. He is too soft and lets her get away with things. I have to live with her.

The majority of partners/carers, however, gave answers which reflected the profound effect of imprisonment upon their children and the punishing impact upon the whole family. For example:

> We didn't expect him to be convicted – it was his first offence. So we didn't prepare the children which, in hindsight, we regret. The children were very shocked, confused and upset. For a long time, none of them could understand what was happening. Schooling hasn't been too badly affected yet as it happened just before their summer holidays. The children haven't told their friends but I suspect everyone knows because it was in the local papers. Neighbours have been hostile, and are constantly complaining about the children, which increases the pressure on them. I seem to be moaning at them all the time which, I realise, isn't helpful.

His dad used to take him to football and swimming. Some friends ask him where his dad is, and he says he's working away, but he's always looking at me as if to say 'What shall I say? Shall I tell them?'

I have no sympathy with fathers who break the law. They shouldn't do the crime. It's the women and kids who suffer and we haven't done anything wrong. It's us that just have to cope with everything – look after the kids, pay the bills. They have it easy; he loves it here, football, mates and he gets paid. Then they expect to just come out and take over. They expect the kids to love them but how can they? They hardly know them. They haven't been around.

These comments by parents clearly express the anguish of many of these children who have been separated from their fathers. The last quote, however, also illustrates the anger of one partner (who is by no means alone) that the inmate is relieved of responsibility during sentence while she is burdened with it all. A means to punish offenders (the necessity for which partners, for the most part, have little quarrel with), without removing them completely from their families, would be greatly welcomed by most.

Sentencing considerations

Again, in illustrative quotations, some considered that sentencing policy should take into account those who have children.

Tagging would be a better idea – or placing a curfew on offenders. It puts a lot of pressure on children having a father in prison. They have to grow up overnight. It's particularly difficult for teenage boys because they need a male figure.

They ought to take into account the nature of the offence and if a man has children before sentencing. If possible community service or other punishments should be given. This has punished us [wife and children] more than him. I have lost my job and our house, and the children have suffered enormously.

These suggestions that community service (recently renamed 'community punishment', under the provisions of the Criminal Justice and Court Services Act 2000) should be more widely used, while tagging and curfews could be substituted, is interesting in the light of the new provision for home detention curfews for some prisoners who may now be released early and electronically tagged at home under sections 99 and 100 of the Crime and Disorder Act 1998.

As noted at the beginning of this volume, however, it would clearly be extremely controversial for criminal justice policy to move towards singling out offenders for more lenient treatment because they were fathers needing to retain a relationship with their children. Most prisoners and partners recognise this, but would nevertheless welcome at least some attention being afforded to the issue at the time of sentencing, in the way which frequently occurs in respect of offending mothers. It is also the case that in some prisons women are allowed to have their infant children living with them up to the age of 2 years. Imprisoned fathers do not have access to parallel facilities, should such an arrangement appear to be in the best interests of the child.

Improving father–child contact arrangements

Within their suggestions for improvement in visiting arrangements, partners also reinforced the importance for them and their children of non-face-to-face contact, particularly phone calls. Privacy during calls and visits was a regular plea; placing inmates in prisons nearer to their homes was another. Here are some examples from a long list:

> More phone calls; a crèche for small children; an outside phone number where families could phone once a week and be connected to the prisoner. Not only does the prisoner sometimes get desperate to talk to their family, so does the family/partner sometimes get desperate to talk to them. There is no facility for this, but could it be a possibility?

> More phone cards; an area for children to play with their dad.

> We should be allowed to have visits in a private room where we can discuss things without being overheard. They ought to try to make the visits more friendly, less like prison. I feel awful bringing my daughter [aged eight months] here; it's not a nice place to bring children. (This was the partner's first visit for three months because she and the inmate had fallen out)

> The phones should be made more private. Often they are situated outside noisy or public areas so it is difficult to have private

conversations or for him to hear what his child is saying. Families who have to travel long distances should get more family visits, or be able to trade in ordinary visits for family visits. There should also be children's food on family visits, e.g. fish fingers, burgers, chips.

They should put people in prisons near their home and think about kids making long journeys on public transport, on hot days, etc. Especially young children.

They tend to assume that all prisoners are bad fathers, but I don't suppose they are much different to anyone else. They don't stop caring about their children because they are inside. They ought to let them have stamps and phone cards; if they really wanted them to maintain family ties then they would.

Again, the theme of needing to strengthen family ties during imprisonment is apparent. One obvious way to improve on the present set of arrangements would certainly be for prisoners to be housed within reasonable travelling distance of their own homes. This idea has been mooted by successive governments but never seriously implemented. A change in allocation criteria which prioritises geographical proximity to home should not, apart from considerations surrounding dangerous prisoners, be impossible to bring about.

Reinforcing formal support schemes

Staff interviewed for the present research also made some suggestions about the formal support schemes in which they were involved. All were concerned about the fact that the schemes were highly dependent on their own continuing involvement. They felt that responsibility should be more firmly integrated into the prison centrally, perhaps in one person's functional role, especially in the light of the family ties ethos of Prison Service Standing Order no. 5, mentioned earlier. However, the 1997 'consolidation' of this order (see Chapter 4) did emphasise increasing security considerations. Staff were mindful that prisons have a major responsibility in this field, though felt that a better balance could be struck through good liaison processes if they were given the time for this. Staff from visits schemes were conscious of the need for better publicity within the prisons and of the extra time and cost for families travelling to them, as well as loss of school and work time. They did not have the time to attend to these problems and needed more support to resource their schemes more effectively. A telephone helpline was one suggestion (and these are in fact beginning to spring up via charitable trusts). Staff from parenting programmes succeeded better in their publicity strategies, but needed the resources to make their programmes available to more participants.

Respondents' views summarised

In summary, the themes arising from respondent suggestions for improvements in supporting the father's parenting role are as follows:

1. Inmates feel they will have more to offer as fathers if they are afforded better access to education and employment training both in prison and after release.

2. Better access to services which support specific need, such as counselling and alcohol/drug rehabilitation is required.

3. Family ties should be strengthened, not reduced, while fathers are in prison; since this is also in the interests of reducing recidivism, prisons could take some responsibility for this by appointing a member of staff to oversee this aspect of prison life. Telephone helplines would be an invaluable resource to staff and families.

4. Sentencing policy should take into account the needs of offenders' children and consider wider use of community service. Weekend imprisonment would be a positive innovation, and the new home detention curfews allowing for early prisoner release should be of help here. The housing of prisoners much closer to their home areas would facilitate closer and more regular contact.

5. It is important not to overlook the fact that a small minority of children are better without contact with their imprisoned fathers.

6. Most respondents, including notably the children themselves, feel that the child–father relationship would benefit from longer and more frequent contact, if this could be built into existing prison visits and telephone contact, with the addition of more town visits and home leave.

7.   Staff running formal support schemes need to be better resourced in order to engage in activity such as publicity and practical assistance to families which will shore up their schemes. Central prison responsibility, again perhaps enshrined in a particular person, would help to ensure the continuation of support schemes if the existing 'product champions' were to move on.

8.   All are conscious of the need for security constraints but feel that these can potentially be dealt with through good liaison between key personnel.

These ideas, most of them realistic and based on knowledge and experience, would certainly be worth incorporating into reviews of policy and programme development.

Healthy child–father relationships and the penal system

Imprisoned fathers comprise a group of absent fathers among whom many will return to live with their family. Our concern has been primarily to focus upon those children and fathers whose relationships are continuing during the prison sentence, though much work remains to be done to assist the maintenance of relationships where contact has otherwise lapsed or is in danger of doing so. While a minority of those interviewed were intending not to reunite ultimately, the evidence from this and other studies is that very many prisoner fathers clearly welcomed the prospect and possibility it afforded for a renewal of stability, solvency and normality. While a significant minority in our study emphasised their 'play' role with children, the majority of fathers looked forward simply to 'being with' their children again on release. Most also wanted to repeat with their own children their positive experiences of being fathered and to avoid repeating their negative ones. This bears out research which has moved on from role characterisation of fathers (often a 'deficit' model in the case of absent fathers) to the notion of generative fathering – i.e. caring for and contributing to the life of the next generation.

Much research on fatherhood has shown the potential importance to children of their fathers, both directly in interactive relationships and indirectly through support to and co-caring with a child's mother. Unfortunately, there is also evidence that, at an extreme, the criminal justice and penal systems constitute a damaging experience for children. In the cause of justice to victims, the protection of society and retribution for offenders, parents are forcibly separated from each other (often for long periods). Fathers are forcibly separated from their children (usually for periods which, to a young child, can seem almost eternal). Seeing their father in prison will often involve children in a lengthy, uncomfortable and boring journey which ends in one hour or so spent in an alien environment where frequently the child cannot touch or be touched by his or her father. On this visit the child might find nothing provided for his/her age group and might have been searched en route to the visits hall. For many children the reality of ordinary visits is depressing and frustrating. In very many ways the system damages the child–parent relationship rather than supports parents. However, there is another side.

Developing visits schemes

Our research shows that there are prison establishments – though very much a minority – where children and parents feel valued and helped. Relationship-enhancing opportunities for children and other family members are provided through children's/family visits schemes, despite the institution's understandable concerns for security and the passing of drugs. There is recognition that children also have needs and that steps can be taken to assist them, in line with Prison Service Standing Orders. Children's and family visits schemes have been found to be feasible and welcome, as well as motivating and humanising of family and inmate. Although since our study was completed a small number of these schemes have been developed in young offender institutions, they need to become just as widespread as the parenting courses in those establishments. Indeed, as a measure of extra support for these young fathers, there is a strong argument for making the two sets of facilities much more closely integrated.

A psychological presence

In respect of non-face-to-face contact, our research showed the importance of relationship maintenance between children and fathers through letters and phone calls, and even for some through audio/video tapes. Some inmates reported regular correspondence with their children and many told of very frequent phone contact. By these means, physically absent fathers were able to sustain a psychological presence in their children's lives – where finance and availability of phones permitted. Children and partners alike confirmed the beneficial effects of such a presence. In this context it is encouraging to note initiatives such as the 'Story Book Dad' scheme in which men taperecord stories for their children. All contacts, whether direct or indirect, are clearly of great importance to children and all other participants; all could benefit from significant reinforcement.

Family ties: a central constituent

Many of our respondents strongly expressed the view that family ties should be strengthened, not reduced, while fathers are in prison. Since this is also in the interests of reducing recidivism, prisons could take some responsibility for this by appointing a supervisor to oversee this aspect of prison life. This is particularly important because the viability of existing children's and family visits schemes and often of parenting/fatherhood courses tends to depend on the enthusiasm and commitment of the leading personnel who, particularly in the case of visits schemes, tend to come from the voluntary/charitable sector. It could also afford the possibility of building external evaluation into schemes/courses to assess their value to children and to prisoner rehabilitation, a constituent frequently missing from these initiatives.

Fatherhood/parenting courses: effects on adults and young offenders

About 30 per cent of adult inmates and 80 per cent of the young offenders in this stratified sample had attended a fatherhood/parenting course. The majority of each group could itemise some of what they had learned, particularly about baby-care skills and child development, and reported that the course had changed the way they perceived the fathering role. This was a very notable development in relation to young offender fathers who, almost universally, spoke positively about the experience and about their desire to be good fathers to their children. Additionally, of those who were in contact with their children, some had overcome complex and adverse circumstances in order to put their children's interests first and ensure that the relationship continued.

However, it was of concern that just over half of young offender fathers in this study received no visits from their children. Partly this related to geographical and travelling constraints, but for the most part was a product of fragmented relationships with the children's mothers. Some of the babies/small children had never seen their fathers; other children had been taken into local authority care; one had been adopted without his father's consent. Nevertheless, half this group had attended parenthood courses. This good intention clearly has the potential to be translated into a reality which is beneficial for both children and young parents. As other research on this issue has also observed (Dennison and Lyon 2001), it is an obvious area for intensive professional intervention and support.

The children's voice

All the children interviewed in our study were in ongoing contact with their prisoner fathers and positive about the continuation of these relationships during the prison sentence and beyond. However, all of them also expressed sadness or distress of some kind and, in common with other research findings (Brown 2001), did not find conventional contact arrangements conducive to the important process of actually developing these relationships in the prison setting. By way of indirect confirmation, the children of at least half of inmate and partner/carer respondents were reported to have presented more difficult behaviour at home following father's imprisonment. Further, children's views suggest that parents underestimate the problems for children in coping with the knowledge of their father's imprisonment in the school setting. Among the implications for schools is their need for clear strategies for the provision of support and trusted teacher-confidants to children in this situation.

These findings suggest that prisoners' children, like any other children in society, need to find a voice and someone who will listen to them. This book began by listing their civil rights, but those rights mean little if children's presence in society is not properly asserted and they are not full social participants. To participate, they require the necessary information, in a language they can understand, to help them make decisions about whether, how and when to be in contact with their imprisoned fathers. While to some extent this information may usefully be in written or electronic form, children's participation may also, depending on age, require a listening advocate who can later represent them in decision-making settings.

Where children are able to express their views directly, it is necessary for those interacting with them to appreciate that the language they use to describe how they feel about having a father in prison, and being in contact with him, may well be different from that used by adults. The challenge here to adults, particularly those located within the penal system, is to create the time, space and facility to ensure that their language is interpreted correctly. This is an important way in which children will learn about justice and mutual respect, about negotiating paths through complex and possibly unhappy circumstances. It is particularly necessary for children in risk situations, who may need special, non-labelling support through a major episode in their lives such as coping with having a parent in prison. This should be taken into account in any plans to develop family support networks, research programmes and media links. In this way, stereotypical representations of children's capacities and likely views may be avoided, and their actual views and experiences taken into account, as and when policies which may impinge on their well-being are under consideration.

As Brown's (2001) study strongly advocates through the words of a teenage child of an imprisoned parent, 'Someone should ask me what it is like for *me!*' This authenticity clearly highlights the centrality of children's views in a situation where adults make decisions for them which affect their lives in a far-reaching fashion. In line with some of the suggestions above, Brown's research found that children of prisoners would benefit from access to information, to a support person and to better and more consistent visiting procedures:

Within the prison estate they are powerless and reduced to a security risk assessment; within the broader community they are silent and silenced. (Brown 2001, p.71)

One of the 26 recommendations for improvement in the report reads as follows:

Issues for children and young people with an imprisoned family member should be incorporated into existing training programmes for teachers, social workers, police and probation officers, health workers and voluntary agencies. (Brown 2001, p.73)

As our own and other research has shown, society is still a long way from bringing about such a development.

Agency links and support networks

A striking feature of our study, supported by other cited research, was that a majority of partners/carers, adult inmates and a third of young offenders reported no links with helping agencies though, for a minority, this was from preference. Although a majority of young offenders, over a third of adult inmates and a fifth of partners had links with their home-based probation service (not infrequently described as unhelpful), it was clear that the majority of parent respondents did not receive help from, turn to or know about organisations which might support them during this critical period in their lives. As outlined at the end of Chapter 6, there is a very clear need for a co-ordinated development of formal and informal support systems, integrated with policy development and informed by research.

The evidence would suggest that a proactive support endeavour on the part of all involved agencies is now required. This would entail seeking out and helping the families of prisoners, showing sensitivity to their particular problems of coping, of relating to the prisoner, of (often) negative previous experiences of welfare organisations, and to the specialised needs of these children. It would also, perhaps, contain a challenge to show how their activities are geared to the inclusion of fathers (as well as mothers) in their family support initiatives. Imprisoned fathers, their children, their partners or their child carers all have very particular needs which, if they are met, may help them to cope independently with the disadvantaged circumstances for relationship development in which they find themselves. Some of the integrated US support programmes are an example here, but they too need continuing financial and public support for their sustenance.

The enhancement of public understanding

The public is justifiably concerned about and sometimes fearful of prisons, prisoners and of all those associated with them. They need to understand that to ascribe negative labels to prisoners' families, and their children in particular, is not to solve the problem but rather to perpetuate it. The fact that an offender may nonetheless be a loving parent, with whom a child wishes to continue a fundamentally important relationship, needs to be explained in straightforward language so that members of society are furnished with some guidance as to the part they can play in supporting such children, thereby reducing the potential for their social exclusion with all its attendant dangers.

Public relations have never been the strong suit of the criminal justice system. There is much talk of community involvement, but little is said about strategies for involving the public with the criminal justice agencies in a way which works towards common interests and goals. Both statutory and voluntary agencies, particularly at local level, could work to inform the public in a variety of ways about the importance for long-term community safety of supporting the reintegration into their families and communities of prisoners who have been released. This would also involve discussing with the public the action that each sector can appropriately take, in order to inculcate a sense of community responsibility and ownership.

At a national level facts and figures provided by research in this field should be widely publicised with an emphasis upon the serious rather than the salacious aspects of the findings. Guidance as to how the public might helpfully respond could accompany such a measure. Perhaps most importantly people should be encouraged to regard and treat prisoners' families as human beings in need of compassion and understanding.

Research and planning implications

In the interests both of the future emotional stability of prisoners' children and of discovering more about the links between sustained family relationships and subsequent reoffending, it is apparent that further research, probably in longitudinal form, needs to be conducted. It would be valuable to know, for example, how prisoners returning to their families are helped to assume the role of responsible parent at home – to the best advantage of their children. The acquisition of such knowledge is fundamental if the surrounding problems identified in this volume are to be effectively tackled. What is required is a full integration of research programmes into the process of policy formulation and application in the criminal justice system, with particular attention to the vulnerability of children and young persons who by default become embroiled in that system.

It is further suggested that mutual feedback between research and policy is especially important. When the evolving role of fatherhood and the changing forms and dimensions of crime are considered alongside the characteristics of the stages of childhood and adolescence, this is obviously true. Policy and practice must not stagnate but should keep abreast of such changes by ensuring that they are informed through research which takes account not only of statistics, systems and processes, but of the views of responsible professionals, victims and the offenders' children and their families. Equally, it should not be too much to hope that such a research framework could feed into international networks, so that action can be informed by successes and failures elsewhere without unnecessary duplication. In this way the formal response to the whole process and meaning of imprisonment and to those affected can remain sufficiently dynamic to pinpoint preventative measures, and devise assessment and intervention techniques relevant to the complexities of contemporary culture.

Conclusion

The findings from this review of the circumstances surrounding continuing contact between imprisoned fathers and their children have highlighted one of society's important dilemmas. On the one hand there is the need for retribution and punishment of lawbreakers, coupled with the protection of the community and justice for victims. On the other hand, there are the rights and needs of children to sustain contact and, by that means, loving, meaningful relationships with their incarcerated fathers. In face of the fact that these needs are in conflict, there is as always a balance to be struck. The research findings suggest that many of the arrangements for child–father contact fall far short of the best examples which we know operate in some prisons, for a minority of prisoners. If all provision for meeting children's contact needs were to be optimised, then the balance would have to shift in the children's favour. Certainly, that has been the expressed desire of the fathers, partners/carers and children endeavouring to maintain their loving familial relationships within and across the prison setting.

The time is long overdue for the children of prisoners to receive a higher priority, and for the prison system to adjust accordingly. The importance of children's stable development needs to be enhanced by a prison system which seeks to exploit every opportunity to offer child and family support, and to encourage a more co-ordinated approach to the endeavour by involving all relevant agencies. This could lead to prisoners accepting more responsibility for their offending, and its impact on their children and families. Additionally, it could promote a fuller public understanding of the value, both social and economic, of rehabilitation following punishment and of well-supported families as a resource in that process. Not only is this in the interests of the children and parents concerned, but clearly it is also to the long-term benefit of the wider society in which we live.

References

Ahrons, C.R. (1983) 'Predictors of paternal involvement post divorce: Mothers' and fathers' perceptions.' *Journal of Divorce, 6*, 55–59.

Ainsworth, M.D.S. (1979) 'Attachment as related to mother–infant interaction.' In J.S. Rosenblatt, R.A. Hinde, C. Beer and M. Busnel (eds) *Advances in the Study of Behaviour.* New York: Academic Press.

Amira, Y. (1992) 'We are not the problem: Black children and their families within the criminal justice system.' In R. Shaw (ed) *Prisoners' Children: What Are the Issues?* London: Routledge.

Anderson, D., Basson, J., Blackstock, K., Buyers, T., Creighton, A., Gill, K., Hall, R., Maclean, M., McTaggart, M. and Pearce, J. (1992) 'Health, social and educational needs of parents and children affected by imprisonment in Scotland.' In R. Shaw (ed) *Prisoners' Children: What Are the Issues?* London: Routledge.

Arendell, T. (1992) 'After divorce: Investigations into father absence.' *Gender and Society, 6*, 4, 562–586.

Arendell, T. (1995) *Fathers and Divorce.* London: Sage.

Barker, R.W. (1994) *Lone Fathers and Masculinities.* Aldershot: Avebury.

Bayse, D.J., Allgood, S.M. and Van Wyk, P.H. (1991) 'Family life education: An effective tool for prisoner rehabilitation.' *Family Relations, 40*, 254–257.

Bertoia, C. and Drakich, J. (1993) 'The father's rights movement: Contradictions in rhetoric and practice.' *Journal of Family Issues, 14*, 180–185.

Biller, H.B. (1993) *Fathers and Families: Paternal Factors in Child Development.* Westport, CT: Auburn House.

Bisnaire, L., Firestone, D. and Rynard, D. (1990) 'Factors associated with academic achievement in children following parental separation.' *American Journal of Orthopsychiatry, 60*, 1, January, 67–76.

Black, D. (1992) 'Children of parents in prison.' *Archives of Disease in Childhood, 67*, 967–970.

Blake, J. (1991) *Sentenced by Association.* London: Save the Children.

Blankenhorn, D. (1995) *Fatherless America: Confronting our most Urgent Social Problem.* New York: Basic Books.

Boswell, G. (1996) *Young and Dangerous: The Backgrounds and Careers of Section 53 Offenders.* Aldershot: Avebury.

Bowlby, J. (1951) *Maternal Care and Mental Health.* Geneva: World Health Organization.

Bowlby, J. (1969) *Attachment and Loss Vol. 1: Loss, Sadness and Depression.* London: Hogarth Press.

Bowlby, J. (1973) *Attachment and Loss Vol. 11: Separation Anxiety and Anger.* London: Hogarth Press.

Bowlby, J. (1980) *Attachment and Loss Vol. 111: Loss, Sadness and Depression.* London: Hogarth Press.

Bradshaw, J. and Millar, J. (1991) *Lone Parent Families in the U.K.* Research Report no. 6, Department of Social Security. London: HMSO.

Brandon, M. and Lewis, A. (1996) 'Significant harm and children's experiences of domestic violence.' *Child and Family Social Work, 1,* 1, 33–42.

Braver, S.L., Fitzpatrick, P.J. and Bay, R. C. (1991) 'Noncustodial parents' report of child support payment.' *Family Relations, 40,* 180–185.

Brodsky, S. (1975) *Families and Friends of Men in Prison: The Uncertain Relationship.* Lexington, MA: Lexington Books.

Brown, G., Harris, T. and Bifulco, A. (1986) 'Long term effects of early loss of parent.' In M. Rutter, E. Carroll, P. Izard and P. Read (eds) *Depression in Young People.* New York: Guilford Press.

Brown, K. (2001) *No-one's Ever Asked Me: Young People with a Prisoner in the Family.* London: FPFSG (Federation of Prisoners' Families Support Groups).

Burgess, A. (1997) *Fatherhood Reclaimed: The Making of the Modern Father.* London: Vermillion.

Burgess, A. and Ruxton, S. (1996) *Men and their Children: Proposals for Public Policy.* London: Institute for Public Policy Research.

Burghes, L., Clarke, L. and Cronin, N. (1997) *Fathers and Fatherhood in Britain.* London: Family Policy Studies Institute.

Caddle, D. (1991) *Parenthood Training for Young Offenders: An Evaluation of Courses in Young Offender Institutions.* RPU Paper no. 63. London: Home Office.

Cadoret, R.J., Troughton, E., O'Gorman, T.W. and Heywood, E. (1985) 'Genetic and environmental factors in major depression.' *Journal of Affective Disorders, 9,* 155–164.

Campion, M.J. (1995) *Who's Fit to be a Parent?* London: Routledge.

Catan, L. (1989) 'The development of young children in HMP mother and baby units.' *Home Office Research Bulletin, 26,* 9–12.

Catan, L., Dennison, C. and Coleman, J. (1997) *Getting Through: Effective Communication in the Teenage Years.* Brighton: Trust for the Study of Adolescence and the BT Forum.

Chapman, T. and Hough, M. (1998) *Evidence Based Practice. A Guide to Effective Practice.* London: HM Inspectorate of Probation, Home Office.

Codd, H. (1998) 'Prisoners' families: The "forgotten victims".' *Probation Journal, 45,* 3, 148–154.

Council of Ministers of the European Communities (1992) *Recommendation on Childcare.* 92/241/EEC of 31 March, OJ L123, 8 May.

Cunningham, S. and Bryson, S. (1997) 'The effects on the child of parental imprisonment.' In NEPACS, *The Child and the Prison: Proceedings of a Conference held at Grey College, Durham*, 85–89. Durham: NEPACS.

Danzinger, S.K. and Radin, D. (1990) 'Absent does not equal uninvolved: Predictors of fathering in teen mother families.' *Journal of Marriage and the Family, 52*, 636–642.

Davis, L. (1983) 'A web of punishment.' *Social Work Today, 14*, 48, 21.

Dennis, N. and Erdos, G. (1992) *Families without Fatherhood*. London: Institute of Economic Affairs, Health and Welfare Unit.

Dennison, C. and Lyon, J. (2001) *Young Offenders, Fatherhood, and the Impact of Parenting Training*. Brighton: Trust for the Study of Adolescence.

Ditchfield, J. (1994) 'Family ties and recidivism: main findings from the literature.' *Home Office Research Bulletin, 36*, 3–9.

Doherty, W.J. (1991) 'Beyond reactivity and the deficit model of manhood: A commentary on articles by Napier, Pittman and Gottman.' *Journal of Marital and Family Therapy, 17*, 29–32.

Drill, R.L. (1986) 'Young adult children of divorced parents: Depression and the perception of loss.' *Journal of Divorce, 10*, 1, 2.

Dyregrov, A. (1994) 'Childhood bereavement: Consequences and therapeutic approaches.' *ACCP Review & Newsletter, 16*, 4, 173–182.

Erikson, E.H. (1950) *Childhood and Society*. New York: Norton.

Erikson, E.H. (1959) *Identity and the Life Cycle*. New York: Norton.

Evans, J. (1998) *Parenting in an Adult Male Prison: A Multi-Agency Project*. Norwich: Norwich Community Health Partnership NHS Trust, Ormiston Children and Families Trust, The Queen's Nursing Institute, HM Prison Service.

Farrington, D.P. (1995) 'The development of offending and anti-social behaviour from childhood: Key findings from the Cambridge Study in Delinquent Development.' *Journal of Child Psychology and Psychiatry, 36*, 6, 929–964.

Ferri, E. (1976) *Growing Up in a One-parent Family*. Slough: NFER.

Fishman, L.T. (1981) 'Losing a loved one to incarceration: The effect of imprisonment on family members.' *Personnel and Guidance Journal, 59*, 372–375.

Fishman, L.T. (1983) 'The impact of incarceration on children of offenders.' *Journal of Children in Contemporary Society, 15*, 89–99.

Fishman, L.T. (1984) 'Women at the wall: a study of prisoners' wives doing time on the outside.' Unpublished PhD thesis. McGill University, Montreal.

FPFSG (Federation of Prisoners' Families Support Groups) (1998) *Newsletter*, 11, Winter.

FPFSG (Federation of Prisoners' Families Support Groups) (1999) *Annual Review 1998–1999*. London: FPFSG.

Freud, S. (1940) 'An outline of psychoanalysis.' In J. Strachey (ed and trans) *The Standard Edition of the Complete Psychological Works of Sigmund Freud, Vol. 23*. London: Hogarth Press, pp.137–207.

Furstenberg, F.F. Jr. (1995) 'Fathering in the inner city: paternal participation and public policy.' In W. Marsiglio (ed) *Fatherhood: Contemporary Theory, Research and Social Policy*. Thousand Oaks, CA: Sage.

Gabel, S. (1992) 'Children of incarcerated and criminal parents: Adjustment, behavior, and prognosis.' *Bulletin of the American Academy of Psychiatry and the Law, 20,* 33–45.

Gamer, E. and Schrader, A. (1981) 'Children of incarcerated parents: problems and interventions.' In R. Stuart and L. Abt (eds) *Children of Separation and Divorce: Management and Treatment.* London: Van Nostrand Reinhold.

Geiger, B. (1996) *Fathers as Primary Caregivers.* Westport, CT: Greenwood Press.

Ghate, D. and Daniels, A. (1997) *Talking about My Generation. A Survey of 8–15 Year-Olds Growing up in the 1990s.* London: NSPCC.

Glaser, D. (1964) *The Effectiveness of a Prison Parole System.* Indianapolis, IN: Bobbs-Merrill.

Glueck, S. and Glueck, E.T (1945) *After-conduct of Discharged Offenders.* London: Macmillan.

Glueck, S. and Glueck, E.T. (1968) *Delinquents and Nondelinquents in Perspective.* Oxford: Oxford University Press.

Greif, G.L. and Kritall, J. (1993) 'Common themes in a group of noncustodial parents.' *Families in Society, 74,* 240–245.

Haarter, G. and Moerings, M. (1991) 'Buiten de muren: tien jaar vereniging relaties von gedetineerden.' *Process, 5,* 115–122.

Haines, K. (1990) *After-care Services for Released Prisoners: A Review of the Literature.* London: HMSO.

Hairston, C.F. (1988) 'Family ties during imprisonment: Do they influence future criminal activity?' *Federal Probation 53,* 48–53

Hairston, C.F. (1989) 'Men in prison: Family characteristics and parenting views.' *Journal of Offender Counseling Services and Rehabilitation, 14,* 1.

Hairston, C.F. (1995) 'Fathers in prison.' In D. Johnson and K. Gables (eds) *Children of Incarcerated Parents.* Lexington, MA: Lexington Books.

Hairston, C.F. (1998) 'The forgotten parent: Understanding the forces that influence incarcerated fathers' relationships with their children.' *Child Welfare: Journal of Policy, Practice and Program, 77,* 617–639, special issue.

Hairston, C.F. and Lockett, P.W. (1987) 'Parents in prison: new directions for social services.' *Social Work,* March/April, 162–164.

Halsey, A.H. (1992) Foreward in N. Dennis and G. Erdos *Families without Fatherhood.* London: Institute of Economic Affairs, Health and Welfare Unit.

Hannon, G., Martin, D. and Martin, M. (1984) 'Incarceration in the family: Adjustment to change.' *Family Therapy, 11,* 253–260.

Hansen, S.M.H. (1986) 'Parent–child relationships in single-father families.' In R.A. Lewis and R.E. Salt (eds) *Men in Families.* Newbury Park: Sage.

Hardwick, D. (1986) *Serving the Second Sentence.* Harborne: Peper Publications.

Hawkins, A.J., Christiansen, S.L., Sargent, K.P. and Hill, E.J. (1993) 'Rethinking fathers' involvement in child care: a developmental perspective.' *Journal of Family Issues, 14,* 4, 531–549.

Hawkins, A.J. and Dollahite, D.C. (1997) 'Beyond the role – inadequacy perspective of fathering.' In A.J. Hawkins and D.C. Dollahite (eds) *Generative Fathering: Beyond Deficit Perspectives.* London: Sage.

Heath, D.T. and McKenry, P.C. (1993) 'Adult family life of men who fathered as adolescents.' *Families in Society, 74,* 36–45.

HM Prison Service (1995) *Directory of Help Agencies: A Guide for Prison Establishments.* London: Prisoner Services Throughcare Section, Abell House.

HM Prison Service (1998) *Visitors Centre Good Practice Guidelines.* Information and Practice 3/1998. London: Sentence Planning Section: Abell House.

Holt, N. and Miller, D. (1972) *Explorations in Inmate Family Relationships.* Research Report no. 46. Sacramento, CA: Californian Dept. of Corrections.

Holwerda, G. (1994) *Mentorprojekt voor Kinderen van Gedetineerden.* Hertogenbosch: Nederlandse Federatie van reclasseringsinstellingen.

Home Office (1991) *Report into Prison Disturbances April 1990 by the Right Honourable Lord Woolf and His Honour Judge Stephen Tumin.* Cmd 1456. London: HMSO.

Home Office (2001) *Occupation of Prisons, Remand Centres, Young Offender Institutions and Police Cells England and Wales 31 March 2001.* London: Research, Development and Statistics Directorate – Offenders and Corrections Unit.

Horner, C. (1994) *The Outsiders: A Survival Guide for Prisoners' Partners and Families.* Belfast: NIACRO.

Hostetter, E. and Jinnah, D. (1993) *Families of Adult Prisoners.* Washington, DC: Prison Fellowship Ministries.

Hounslow, B., Stephenson, A., Stewart, J. and Crancher, J. (1982) *Children of Imprisoned Parents.* Sydney: Ministry of Youth and Community Services of New South Wales.

Howe, D. (1995) *Attachment Theory for Social Work Practice.* London: Macmillan.

Ihinger-Tallman, M., Pasley, K. and Buehler, C. (1995) 'Developing a middle-range theory of father involvement postdivorce.' In W. Marsiglio (ed) *Fatherhood: Contemporary Theory, Research and Social Policy.* London: Sage.

Johnson, D.J. (1997) *Father Presence Matters: A Review of the Literature. Towards an Ecological Framework of Fathering and Child Outcomes.* Philadephia: National Center on Fathers and Families.

Johnson, T., Selber, K. and Lauderdale, M. (1998) 'Developing quality services for offenders and families: An innovative partnership.' *Child Welfare: Journal of Policy, Practice and Program, 77,* 595–615, special issue.

Kiselica, M., Rotzien, A. and Doms, J. (1994) 'Preparing teenage fathers for parenthood: A group psychoeducational approach.' *Journal for Specialists in Group Work, 19,* 83–94.

Kruk, E. (1991) 'Discontinuity between pre- and post-divorce father–child relationships: New evidence regarding paternal disengagement.' *Journal of Divorce and Remarriage, 16,* 3/4, 195–227.

Lamb, M.E. (1981) 'Fathers and child development.' In M.E. Lamb (ed) *The Role of the Father in Child Development.* New York: Wiley.

Lamb, M.E. (1986) 'The changing role of fathers.' In M.E. Lamb (ed) *The Father's Role: Applied Perspectives.* New York: Wiley.

Lamb, M. (1987) 'The development of father–infant relationships.' In M.E. Lamb (ed) *The Role of the Father in Child Development*, 2nd edn. New York: Wiley.

Lanier, C.S. (1993) 'Affective states of fathers in prison.' *Justice Quarterly, 10,* 49–65.

Leclair, D. (1978) 'Home furlough programme effects on rates of recidivism.' *Criminal Justice and Behaviour, 5,* 249–259.

Lewis, C. and O'Brien, M. (1987) *Re-assessing Fatherhood.* London: Sage.

Lewis, M., Feiring, C. and Weinraub, M. (1981) 'The father as a member of the child's social network.' In M.E. Lamb (ed) *The Role of the Father in Child Development.* New York: Wiley.

Liederman, D. (1998) 'Foreword.' *Child Welfare: Journal of Policy, Practice and Program, 77,* 467–468, special issue.

Light, R. (ed) (1992) *Prisoners' Families: Keeping in Touch.* Bristol: Bristol Centre for Criminal Justice.

Light, R. (1993) 'Why support prisoners' tie groups?' *Howard Journal, 32,* 4, 322–329.

Light, R. (1994) *Black and Asian Prisoners' Families.* Bristol: University of the West of England, Bristol Centre for Criminal Justice.

Lloyd, E. (1992a) 'Prisoners' children: The role of prison visitors' centres.' In R. Shaw (ed) *Prisoners' Children: What are the Issues?* London: Routledge.

Lloyd, E. (ed) (1992b) *Children Visiting Holloway Prison: Inside and Outside Perspectives on the All-day Visits Scheme at HMP Holloway.* London: Save the Children.

Lloyd, E. (1995) *Prisoners' Children: Research, Policy and Practice.* London: Save the Children.

Lloyd, E. (1997) 'Defending the rights of prisoners' children: Principles and practice.' In NEPACS, *The Child and the Prison: Proceedings of a Conference held at Grey College, Durham.* Durham: NEPACS.

Londerville, S. and Main, M. (1981) 'Security of attachment, compliance and maternal training methods in the second year of life.' *Developmental Psychology, 17,* 298–299.

Lowenstein, A. (1986) 'Temporary single parenthood: The case of prisoners' families.' *Journal of Applied Family and Child Study, 35,* 79–85.

McDermott, K. and King, R. (1992) 'Prison rule 102: "Stand by your man": the impact of penal policy on the families of prisoners.' In R. Shaw *Prisoners' Children: What are the Issues?* London: Routledge.

McLanahan, S. and Sandefur, G. (1994) *Growing Up with a Single Parent: What Helps, What Hurts.* Cambridge, MA: Harvard University Press.

Magnusson, D. (1988) *Individual Development from an Interactional Perspective.* London: Lawrence Elbaum Associates.

Mardon, J. (1996) 'A parenting course for young men.' In T. Newburn and G. Mair (eds) *Working with Men.* London: Russell House.

Marsiglio, W. (1995) 'Fathers' diverse life course patterns and roles: Theory and social intervention.' In W. Marsiglio (ed) *Fatherhood: Contemporary Theory, Research and Social Policy.* London: Sage.

Michaud, M. (ed) (1992) *Enfants, Parents, Prison: pour maintenir les relations entre l'enfant et son parent détenu.* Cahiers no. 4. Dijon: Fondation de France.

Millham, S., Bullock, R., Hosie, K. and Haak, M. (1986) *Lost in Care: The Problems of Maintaining Links between Children in Care and their Families.* Aldershot: Gower.

Milligan, C. and Dowie, A. (1998) *What Do Children Need from their Fathers?* Occasional Paper no. 42. University of Edinburgh: Centre for Theology and Public Issues.

Millington, R. (1998) 'The goodfather.' *Prison Service News, 16,* 165, 12–14.

Minton, C. and Pasley, K. (1996). 'Fathers' parenting role identity and father involvement: A comparison of nondivorced and nonresident fathers.' *Journal of Family Issues, 17,* 26–45.

Moore, S. (1988) 'Teachers and prisoners' children.' *Childright, 43,* 16.

Moore, S. (1992) 'A link with normality: The role a school could play to help a prisoner's child in crisis.' In R. Shaw (ed) *Prisoners' Children: What are the Issues?* London: Routledge.

Moore, S. (1997) 'The prisoner's child and the school.' In NEPACS *The Child and the Prison: Proceedings of a Conference at Grey College, Durham.* Durham: NEPACS.

Morris, P. (1965) *Prisoners and their Families.* London: George Allen.

Nash, A. and Hay, D.F. (1993) 'Relationships in infancy as precursors and causes of later relationships and psychopathology.' In D.F. Hay and A. Angold (eds) *Precursors and Causes in Development and Psychopathology.* Chichester: Wiley.

NEPACS (North Eastern Prison After Care Society) (1997) *The Child and the Prison: Proceedings of a Conference held at Grey College, Durham.* Durham: NEPACS.

Noble, C. (1995) *Prisoners' Families: The Every Day Reality.* Ipswich: Ormiston Charitable Trust.

O'Brien, M. and Jones, D. (1996). 'The absence and presence of fathers: Accounts from children's diaries.' In U. Bjornberg and A.K. Kollind (eds) *Men's Family Relations.* Gothenburg: University of Goteborg Publications.

Parish, T.S. (1987) 'Children's self-concepts: Are they affected by parental divorce and remarriage?' *Journal of Social Behaviour and Personality, 2,* 4, 559–562.

Parke, R. (1981) *Fathers.* Cambridge, MA: Harvard University Press.

Parton, C. and Parton, N. (1989) 'Child protection, the law and dangerousness.' In O. Stevenson (ed) *Child Abuse: Public Policy and Professional Practice.* Hemel Hempstead: Harvester Wheatsheaf.

Peart, K. and Asquith, S. (1992) *Scottish Prisoners and their Families: The Impact of Imprisonment on Family Relationships.* Edinburgh: Scottish Forum on Prisons and Families.

Pellegrini, A.M. (1992) 'Coping with a father in prison: The child's perspective.' Paper presented at the Vth European Conference on Developmental Psychology, Seville.

Pellegrini, A.M. (1997) 'Children coping with a father in prison: Psychological tasks.' In NEPACS *The Child and the Prison: Proceedings of a Conference held at Grey College, Durham.* Durham: NEPACS.

Philbrick, D. (1997) 'Child and adolescent mental health and the prisoner's child.' In NEPACS *The Child and the Prison: Proceedings of a Conference held at Grey College, Durham.* Durham: NEPACS.

Pope, V. (1987) 'We all went to prison: The distress of prisoners' children.' *Probation Journal, 34,* 1, 92–96.

Ramsden, S. (1998) *Working with Children of Prisoners: A Resource for Teachers.* London: Save the Children.

Rhoden, J.L. and Robinson, B.E. (1995) 'Teen dads: A generative fathering perspective versus the deficit myth.' In A.J. Hawkins and D.C. Dollahite (eds) *Generative Fathering: Beyond Deficit Perspectives.* London: Sage.

Richards, M.P.M. (1987) 'Children, parents and families: Developmental psychology and the re-ordering of relationships at divorce.' *International Journal of Law and the Family, 1, 2, 295–317.*

Richards, M.P.M. (1989) 'Joint custody revisited.' *Family Law, 19, 83–85.*

Richards, M. (1992) 'The separation of children and parents: Some issues and problems.' In R. Shaw (ed) *Prisoners' Children: What are the Issues?* London: Routledge.

Richards, M.P.M., Dunn, J.F. and Antonis, B. (1977) 'Caretaking in the first year of life.' *Child Development, 48, 167–181.*

Richards, M., McWilliams, B., Allcock, L., Enterkin, J., Owens, P. and Woodrow, J. (1994) *The Family Ties of English Prisoners: The Results of the Cambridge Project on Imprisonment and Family Ties.* Cambridge: Occasional Paper no. 2, Centre for Family Research.

Risman, B. (1989) 'Can men "mother"? Life as a single father.' In B.J. Risman and P. Schwartz (eds) *Gender in Intimate Relationships: A Microstructural Approach.* Belmont, CA: Wadsworth.

Rutter, M. (1981) *Maternal Deprivation Reassessed,* 2nd edn. London: Virago.

Rutter, M. and Giller, H. (1983) *Juvenile Delinquency: Trends and Perspectives.* Harmondsworth: Penguin.

Rutter, M. and Madge, N. (1976) *Cycles of Disadvantage.* London: Heinemann.

Santrock, J.W. and Warshak, R. (1979) 'Father custody and social development in boys and girls.' *Journal of Social Issues, 35,* 113.

Schaffer, H.R. (1990) *Making Decisions about Children.* Oxford: Blackwell.

Seymour, C. (1998) 'Children with parents in prison: Child welfare policy, program and practice issues.' *Child Welfare: Journal of Policy, Practice and Program, 77,* 469–493, special issue.

Seymour, C. and Hairston, C. (eds) (1998) 'Children with parents in prison.' *Child Welfare: Journal of Policy, Practice and Program, 77,* special issue.

Shaw, R. (1987) *Children of Imprisoned Fathers.* London: Hodder and Stoughton.

Shaw, R. (ed) (1992) *Prisoners' Children: What are the Issues?* London: Routledge.

Shaw, R. (1997) 'The child and the prison, 1996 and beyond.' In NEPACS *The Child and the Prison: Proceedings of a Conference held at Grey College, Durham.* Durham: NEPACS.

Shaw, S. and Crook, F. (1991) *Who's Afraid of Implementing Woolf?* London: Prison Reform Trust and Howard League.

Simpson, B., McCarthy, P. and Walker, J. (1995) *Being There: Fathers After Divorce.* Newcastle: Relate Centre for Family Studies, University of Newcastle upon Tyne.

Snarey, J.R. (1993) *How Fathers Care for the Next Generation.* Cambridge, MA: Harvard University Press.

Speake, S., Cameron, S. and Gilroy, R. (1997) *Young Single Fathers: Participation in Fatherhood – Barriers and Bridges.* London: Family Policy Studies Centre.

Stolz, L.M. (1967) *Influences on Parent Behaviour.* London: Tavistock Publications.

United Nations General Assembly (1989) *The Convention on the Rights of the Child.* New York: United Nations.

Walker, N. (1992) 'Introduction: Theory, practice and an example.' In R. Shaw (ed) *Prisoners' Children: What are the Issues?* London: Routledge.

Wallerstein, J. and Blakeslee, S. (1989) *Second Chances: Men, Women and Children a Decade after Divorce.* New York: Ticknor and Fields.

Waters, E., Wippman, J. and Sroufe, L.A. (1979) 'Attachment, positive affect, and competence in the peer group: Two studies in construct validation.' *Child Development, 50,* 821–829.

Wedge, P. (1995) *A Report on Children's Visits to Imprisoned Fathers: The Scheme at HMP Whitemoor.* Ipswich: Ormiston Trust.

Wedge, P. (1996) 'Loss in childhood and paternal imprisonment.' In D. Howe (ed) *Attachment and Loss in Child and Family Social Work.* Aldershot: Avebury.

Weissman, M. and LaRue, C. (1998) 'Earning trust from youths with none to spare.' *Child Welfare: Journal of Policy, Practice and Program, 77,* 579–594, special issue.

West, D.J. (1982) *Delinquency: Its Roots and Career Prospects.* London: Heinemann.

Williams, F. (1998) 'Troubled masculinities in social policy discourses: fatherhood.' In J. Poppay, J. Hearn and J. Edwards (eds) *Men, Gender Divisions and Welfare.* London: Routledge.

Wilson, D. (1996) 'Sentenced to paternal deprivation: Contact between children and their imprisoned fathers.' Unpublished MA dissertation, Norwich: University of East Anglia.

Wilson-Croome, L. (1992) 'Prisoners' families: Should the probation service have a role?' In R. Shaw (ed) *Prisoners' Children: What are the Issues?* London: Routledge.

Woodrow, J. (1992) 'Mothers inside, children outside. What happens to the dependent children of female inmates?' In R. Shaw (ed) *Prisoners' Children: What are the Issues?* London: Routledge.

Subject index

Name index

Ahrons, C.R. 54, 160
Ainsworth, M.D.S. 15, 160
Amira, Y. 23, 160
Anderson, D. et al, 138
Arendell, T. 54, 61, 160

Barker, R.W. 15, 160
Bayse, D.J., Allgood S.M. and Van Wyk, P.H. 27
Bertoia C.J. and Drakich, J. 54
Biller, H.B. 17, 160
Bisnaire, L., Firestone D. and Rynard, D. 53
Black, D. 35, 62, 160, 167
Blake, J. 21, 160
Blankenhorn, D. 55, 161
Boswell, G. 13, 161
Bowlby, J. 13, 15, 30, 161
Bradshaw J. and Millar, J. 52
Brandon, M. 62, 161
Braver, S.L., Fitzpatrick, P.J. and Bay, R.C. 54
Brodsky, S. 21, 161
Brown, K. 138, 154–6, 161
Brown, G., Harris, T. and Bifulco, A. 138
Burgess, A. 19, 52, 161
Burgess, A. and Ruxton, S. 19
Burghes, L. et al, 19, 57
Burghes, L., Clarke, L. and Cronin, N. 14

Caddle, D. 27, 32, 119–20, 123, 126, 162
Caderet, R.J. et al, 138
Campion, M.J. 58, 162
Catan, L. 11, 26, 55, 61, 162
Chapman, T. and Hough, M. 144
Codd, H. 28, 135, 162
Cunningham, S. and Bryson, S. 138

Danzinger, S.K. and Radin, D. 56
Davis, L. 21, 162
Dennis, N. and Erdos, G, 55
Dennison, C. and Coleman, J. 55
Dennison, C. and Lyon, J. 28, 119–20, 123, 131, 154
Ditchfield, J. 23, 162
Doherty, W.J. 17, 162
Drill, R.L. 53, 163
Dyregrov, A. 111, 163

Erikson, E.H. 17, 30, 163
Evans, J. 28, 122, 126, 163

Farrington, D.P. 13, 57, 163
Ferri, E. 53, 163
Fishman, L.T. 21, 163
Freud, S. 15, 163
Furstenberg, F.F., Jnr. 145, 164

Gabel, S. 26, 164
Gamer, E. and Schrader, A. 100
Geiger, B. 16, 164
Ghate, D. and Daniels, A. 19
Giller, H. 56, 170
Glaser, D. 23, 164
Gluecks, 16